WRITING
THE LIFE POETIC

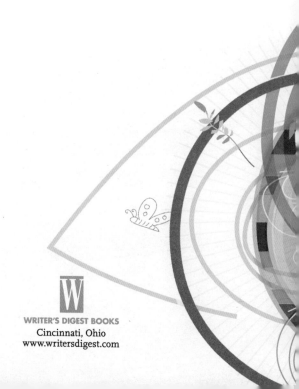

WRITER'S DIGEST BOOKS
Cincinnati, Ohio
www.writersdigest.com

SAGE COHEN

WRITING
THE LIFE POETIC

AN INVITATION TO
READ & WRITE POETRY

Writing the Life Poetic. Copyright © 2009 by Sage Cohen. Manufactured in China. All rights reserved. No other part of this book may be reproduced in any form or by any electronic or mechanical means including information storage and retrieval systems without permission in writing from the publisher, except by a reviewer, who may quote brief passages in a review. Published by Writer's Digest Books, an imprint of F+W Media, Inc., 4700 East Galbraith Road, Cincinnati, Ohio 45236. (800) 289-0963. First edition.

For more resources for writers, visit www.writersdigest.com/books.

To receive a free weekly e-mail newsletter delivering tips and updates about writing and about Writer's Digest products, register directly at http://news letters.fwmedia.com.

13 12 11 10 09   5 4 3 2 1

Distributed in Canada by Fraser Direct, 100 Armstrong Avenue, Georgetown, Ontario, Canada L7G 5S4, Tel: (905) 877-4411. Distributed in the U.K. and Europe by David & Charles, Brunel House, Newton Abbot, Devon, TQ12 4PU, England, Tel: (+44) 1626-323200, Fax: (+44) 1626-323319, E-mail: postmaster@ davidandcharles.co.uk. Distributed in Australia by Capricorn Link, P.O. Box 704, Windsor, NSW 2756 Australia, Tel: (02) 4577-3555.

Library of Congress Cataloging-in-Publication Data
Cohen, Sage.
  Writing the life poetic / Sage Cohen. -- 1st ed.
    p. cm.
  ISBN 978-1-58297-557-3 (pbk. : alk. paper)
  1. Poetry--Authorship. 2. Creative writing. I. Title.
PN1059.A9C63 2009
808.1--dc22   2008045076

media

EDITED BY JANE FRIEDMAN
DESIGNED BY TERRI WOESNER
ILLUSTRATIONS BY GRÉGOIRE VION
PRODUCTION COORDINATED
BY MARK GRIFFIN

DEDICATION

For two great teachers: Albert Cwanger, who believed in me before I believed in myself, and the relentless Matthew Carr, who demanded greatness and launched my love affair with literature.

TABLE OF
CONTENTS

Welcome!

My friend Pam once shared an old Irish proverb with me: "When I count my blessings, I count you twice." In the same way that friendship can be a double blessing, so can a poem. Poetry gives us an opportunity to experience our lives twice. First, as it happens, in real time. And second, in heart time. The poem gives us a kind of cosmic canvas to savor a moment, make sense of it, put a little frame around it, and digest our experience more completely. It also gives us a way to travel profoundly into experiences that are not our own and, if we are lucky, alight on a moment of truth about the human condition every now and then.

Perhaps in reaction to these times of techno-powered turbo speed, a growing number of people are discovering the joy of slowing down to the pleasures and rhythms of their own creative process. If you have always wondered what it would be like to express your thoughts, feelings, observations, or stories in words, this book is for you. If you have found poetry boring, difficult, incomprehensible, or intimidating, this book is for you. If you think poetry sounds fun, but you have no idea how one cultivates a poetic state of mind, this book is for you. If you're already writing poetry and would like to infuse your muse with some invigorating strategies, approaches, and prompts to get your juices flowing, this book is for you.

Welcome to *Writing the Life Poetic*, where we'll be taking poetry off of its academic pedestal and into our lives where it belongs. In these pages you'll find everything you need to start writing, reading, and appreciating poetry in a new way—whatever way pleases and inspires you most. Designed to be a creative companion for poets at all levels, *Writing the Life Poetic* will help you cultivate your craft, be receptive to the poetry around you, practice writing poetry, and find daily delight in all things poetic.

Because some poets write better—or more happily—in good company, we've created a way for readers of *Writing the Life Poetic* to learn and practice together. Join us at www.writingthelifepoetic.typepad.com to share ideas and inspiration with other poets as you travel through this book. Getting support from and feeling connected to a community that shares your passion for living and writing a poetic life can make all the difference. I look forward to seeing you there.

꧁ 1 ꧂
WHY READ AND WRITE POETRY?

"Poetry isn't a profession, it's a way of life. It's an empty basket; you put your life into it and make something out of that."

—Mary Oliver

Last year, I attended a reading of *VoiceCatcher*, a magnificent anthology of women writers from Portland, Oregon. Five women read a range of stories, poetry and essays; at the end of the event, they took questions. An audience member asked, "Why do you write?" Each woman had a different answer:

"To bear witness."

"Because in writing, I can be anyone."

"To stay engaged with my own divinity."

"Unlike life, nothing is permanent in writing. Everything is malleable."

"To open minds and change the world."

I present this small sampling of feedback as a reminder that there may be as many reasons to write as there are writers. Many poets don't know or couldn't articulate what brought them to poetry and what keeps them coming back for more. Some people are not sure if they should even try poetry, whether it's worth the risk. Ultimately, we all have to decide for ourselves why and how we engage poetry. Here are some ways that poets have come to poetry. Perhaps they will inspire you to give it a go.

"Over the years, I've turned to poetry to express feelings and describe experiences, ask questions and draw conclusions—having my say and wanting to be heard. Poetry has stretched me, by challenging my own creative capacity and intellectual boundaries. Poetry has strengthened me, by being there as a friend when I needed to talk and when I needed to listen. It's served as a vessel for my joy and a tonic for my grief."

—Claire Sykes

"Much like Gregory Orr, Poetry is Survival for me, too. I write poetry to investigate social, political and environmental issues. I find that poetry gives me the latitude for self-expression, and helps me take the hard edges of the world and bring them to the surface. After 30 years in helping professions, I am driven to reveal what I know and see about the human condition in a way that provokes critical thought."

—Toni Partington

GENUINE IMITATION | BY WILLA SCHNEBERG

Give me the fake,
the imitation, the simulation, any day
over the real thing.
Give me the bronze garbage
in Haymarket Square
with the inlaid crumpled Boston Globe,
embedded lettuce leaves,
flattened fish scales,
that will never be burned,
bagged or rotted.
Give me the plaster life size cows
black with white spots
shaped like clouds,
in the parking lot outside
the Hilltop Steak House,
who will not experience
the irritation of flies or
the teat sucking machine.
Give me my daughter's model trains
endlessly circling towns
that have no pollution,
everyone's welcome and whoever's
sick goes to the doll hospital.
Give me the poem,
its room not even a page wide,
where one enters as often as one likes
to watch the man place quarters
on his dead wife's lids,
to feel the grief not your own.

BEDSIDE READING | by Paulann Petersen
For Looking Glass Bookstore

The too-soon hour
you emptied by waking

fills with the book you earlier
set aside to fall asleep.

What harm in a few more pages
read long before dawn?

On this lamplight lake, held
in the boat of another's making,

you float—lifted, rocked, stolen away.
Buoyed along in a writer's craft.

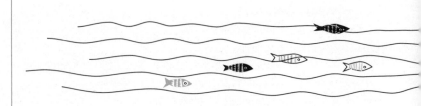

Sharing poetry enables us to give of ourselves and receive others in a way that is often deeper and more complete than what is available to us in conversation. When experiencing others' poems, we are often inspired and instructed about our own capacity to feel, think, know, share, discover. In this way, poetry gives us not only what is specific and unique but also what is common and shared among people. A relationship with poetry can be one of the most life-affirming ways to more intimately know ourselves and more deeply appreciate the universalities of human experience.

> *"Poetry has made me braver. It has given me a place to go when I can't talk to people or I'm not finding the answers. It helps me shed. Once a feeling is locked into a poem it feels solved and over. I started writing as a child. I think it was because I had a lot to digest and was too shy and untrusting to share with people. I really kept to myself and so poetry and writing gave me a place to escape and to talk. Then I started sharing my stuff and getting good feedback. This brought me out of myself and helped me talk, talk louder, and listen better."*

—Brittany Baldwin

In the mid 1990s, I taught poetry at Goldwater Hospital in New York through a program established by the poet Sharon Olds. At this residential hospital, we wrote poems in tandem with people whose bodies were no longer able to write poems on their own. With one woman, who was entirely immobilized except for the use of her eyes, we'd hold up a letterboard and point to one letter at a time until she rolled up her eyes to signify: *Yes! That's the letter I want!* In this way, her poems were written one laborious, glorious word at a time. Poetry gave the residents of Goldwater Hospital and the graduate students who worked with them a shared purpose: the celebration of life through the labor of creating poems. Since that time, every poem I write is in some way for and with those whose life circumstances limit their own writing.

What does poetry mean to you? What particular path has brought you to this moment with this book in your hands? What is it that you would like to discover? What poems are waiting in the wings to move through you? Who might you find yourself to be when you go deeper into the realm of reading and writing poetry?

WHAT MAKES A POEM A POEM?

"Poetry is a relationship with language.
Discovering is part of the process. The
fewer pre-conceived notions, the more
openness, the better the relationship."

—Dan Raphael

In 1964, Supreme Court Justice Potter Stewart famously proclaimed, "I can't define pornography, but I know it when I see it." Many people feel the same way about poetry. It is difficult to summarize what makes a poem a poem, and what the experience of writing poetry might be. Poetry means something different to each of us, and our relationship with it as writers and readers is personal and individual.

And yet, in some ways, a poem is like a meal. There are a finite set of "ingredients" that may go into a meal (vegetables, grains, meats, cheeses, spices) and an infinite number of ways that those ingredients might be combined. Likewise, there is a basic set of ingredients that go into the making of a poem. And just as we know that a shoe does not belong in our chicken soup, there are certain parameters that distinguish poetry from other literary forms. Let's take a look at the most common ingredients we'll find in the poetry pot, and explore how they can be used to create some very diverse feasts.

COMPRESSION
Compression—the art of conveying much with few words—is one of poetry's signatures. While a novel has hundreds of pages to convey the arc of its narrative, a poem typically has anywhere from a few lines to a few pages to do so. This means that every word counts and must be both precise and emotionally alive.

LINES AND STANZAS

Lines and stanzas are two of the easiest ways to distinguish poems from prose. In prose, the sentence is the basic unit of language. In a poem, the line is the basic unit defining the momentum of a narrative. (The prose poem is an exception to this rule.) Where and how a poet breaks a line and groups lines into stanzas influences the speed and rhythm with which the reader takes in the poem. (For more on stanzas, see chapter thirty-four.)

MUSIC

In poetry, language does double duty as both music and content. The rhythms and sounds that words make can have as great an influence on the reader's experience of a poem as the literal meaning (if any) that is conveyed. Some poems employ the strict meter and rhyme patterns that certain forms demand. More common today is the free verse poem in which the poet has an unlimited range of possibilities in expressing music through words. Some poems use language entirely as a musical instrument, without offering any clear narrative at all. (For more on music, see chapter twenty-nine.)

IMAGERY

Poems use imagery to convey our world and our lives in surprising new ways. Rather than tell us what is happening, a poem may simply show us. Through simile and metaphor (described in chapter nineteen), poems line up seemingly unlike things and help us see them anew. This gives the reader an opportunity to come to her own conclusions.

Poetry is an expansive medium with far more possibilities than rules, so there will always be poems that contradict the general ingredients explored above. As you go through this book, write poems, and read the poetry of others, keep your own list of qualities defining what makes a poem. In the short term, this will help you become more conscious of what you're doing and why. Over time, these fundamentals will be imprinted into your being so that the shaping of a poem becomes a natural process.

START WHERE YOU ARE

*"I spent most of my life being a mother and a wife,
so what I had to look at were images around
the house. The moon to me looks like a dinner
plate broken in half, and the clouds look like a
dish towel . . . And of course the moon has been
a symbol for women for centuries and a poetic
image forever. But I try to do something new
with it. That's what a poet does, try to avoid
clichés and reissue a traditional image in a
contemporary way and find a new way to look
at an old thing."*

—Dorianne Laux

Perhaps you envision poets as larger-than-life beings who have extraordinary, magical experiences (and powers) completely unlike any you will ever encounter. You might imagine that a "real" poet lives in complete isolation in a romantic cabin on a pond, or is surrounded by minions in an ivory tower. Could they possibly be driving their kids to soccer practice and hauling out the garbage on Thursday nights like everyone else?

The answer is yes. Poets are regular people who simply take the time to digest their regular, real-life experiences and transform them into poems. Mary Oliver wrote an absolutely brilliant poem about a woman cleaning a public toilet. Ted Kooser wrote a poem in which a man stands in a drug store, contemplating a five-subject notebook (see page 14). What we learn from such examples is that a poem can begin with some tangible thing or observation from our everyday lives, then blossom into a larger exploration of a more esoteric and universal concept, such as aging.

When it comes to writing poetry, the raw material of your life and imagination is more than enough.

Even the lives that appear ordinary on the surface are replete with unnamed wildernesses waiting to be unearthed. When you pay close attention and give voice to what you discover in your everyday life, you are inviting the untapped mysteries of your experience to the surface. The more you write, the more you will come to trust that your ordinary life is extraordinary enough to serve up an endless supply of poems.

Here are a few exercises that can help you tap the poetry in your daily life.

- Choose an activity you do regularly that is the absolutely most routine, unremarkable event of your day. (Mine would be doing dishes.) Write down the answers to these questions about it:

  - Notice the physical feeling of this routine. Which muscles are involved? What kind of rhythm or tempo does it involve? Are you cold or hot, energized or depleted?

  - How do you feel emotionally when you do this?

  - What are the smells associated with this activity? (I use lavender soap, so my sink smells like a French garden.)

  - What do you see when engaged in this routine? (I look out at the butterfly bush and magnolia tree in my backyard. I enjoy watching meals erased from plates and glasses.)

  - Pay close attention to what you are thinking. What images and ideas bubble up as you do this activity?

  - How does the time of day or weather or location (indoors vs. outdoors, your home vs. someone else's home, summer breeze or snowfall) affect your experience?

- What wildlife, plants and trees do you see out your window at home, at work, or en route to work? What do they look like, feel like, sound like? What are their names?

- What are the visual cues and references points you encounter in your home or workspace?

  - Make a list of the twenty things you come into contact with most.

  - Write down something else in the world that each of these twenty things reminds you of. For example: The red teapot reminds me of the robin redbreast. The worn wood of the mirror over the sink reminds me of the door to Grandpa's barn. The curlicue pattern on the silver platter makes me think of storm clouds.

- Think of someone you see regularly in passing but do not know well, such as your mail carrier, barista or neighbor. Write a poem that imagines what his life might be like:

  - Who does he love?

  - What has he lost?

  - What do his pajamas look like?

  - What are his aspirations?

  - What does he eat for breakfast?

A Spiral Notebook | by Ted Kooser

The bright wire rolls like a porpoise
in and out of the calm blue sea
of the cover, or perhaps like a sleeper
twisting in and out of his dreams,
for it could hold a record of dreams
if you wanted to buy it for that,
though it seems to be meant for
more serious work, with its
college-ruled lines and its cover
that states in emphatic white letters,
5 SUBJECT NOTEBOOK. It seems
a part of growing old is no longer
to have five subjects, each
demanding an equal share of attention,
set apart by brown cardboard dividers,
but instead to stand in a drugstore
and hang on to one subject
a little too long, like this notebook
you weigh in your hands, passing
your fingers over its surfaces
as if it were some kind of wonder.

༄ 4 ༄
SHOW VS. TELL:
THE ART OF THE IMAGE

The purpose of a newspaper article is to report the facts of a story objectively and without bias. A poem's job is to bring a story viscerally to life from a particular point of view. In making a poetic scene or a narrative palpable for readers, descriptive images are often far more engaging than statements. This truth has been distilled to a golden rule of poetry that echoes through classrooms everywhere: *Show, don't tell.*

Let's take a look at what show vs. tell means by considering different ways to communicate the concept of "weakness":

Telling: "I felt weak."

Showing: "I could barely lift the spoon to my mouth."

The first example explains to the reader how the speaker feels. The second example gives some specific details to bring the concept of "weak" to life. We can see where weakness lives in the speaker's body in this moment. When you "show" with images, you offer the reader a visual, tactile, sometimes auditory reference, rather than a conceptual one. Because weakness might look and feel completely different in your body than it does in mine, images can help you more effectively articulate your own experience. They can also help move a poem from vague to specific, making it a lot more interesting.

The goal in "showing" is to present a fresh, new image—something that hasn't been said or written previously. If the first thing that comes to mind in "show" mode is something you've heard before, such as "My arms were as limp as noodles," reach farther. Overly familiar phrases may once have had an impact on readers, but through repetition they have lost their potency—and are ultimately demoted to the status of cliché. These unsurprising images will not serve your poem.

Despite what the "show, don't tell" mantra advises, declarative statements are not always bad or unnecessary in poetry. In fact, it is very common for poems to employ a mix of both show and tell to bring an idea to life. For example, in my poem "Like the Heart, the World," I start the second stanza with a declarative "tell" statement:

> It is hard to know how to let go.
> Cloud carries pink like paint
> carries pigment. Each word, too,
> enmeshed in the web of idea.

I elaborate on the statement about letting go using two examples that show entanglements in nature and language. Rather than eliminating all "tell" from our poems, a more useful consideration is how to balance statements and images to create the greatest impact.

A good question to ask yourself every time you make a declarative statement is, "What would happen if I described this instead of naming it?" And consider the opposite: whether your descriptive images could benefit from a phrase of more straightforward explanation. Sometimes, the only way to know is to try out a number of different approaches and see what feels right. This will help you develop your own aesthetic for mixing show and tell in poems.

 **TRY THIS!**

- Rewrite the following statements to "show" instead of "tell":

    - Her hair was a mess.
    - I hate the smell of roses.
    - He couldn't wait to see her again.
    - The preschooler wasn't ready to leave the playground when recess was over.
    - You always change your mind.
    - The moon is full.
    - I refuse to give up.

- Now create a "tell" statement and then a "show" statement for each of these:

WRITING THE LIFE POETIC

- How do you feel about losing a game?
- Describe a moment when a friend did something special for you.
- What's your favorite time of day and why?
- Describe your first (or an early) memory.
- Observe a stranger on the street, and describe his appearance or behavior.
- What is it like to visit with your family?

- Reinvent these clichés using fresh, original language:

  - He has ants in his pants.
  - I feel like a fish out of water.
  - After her shower, she felt fresh as a daisy.
  - It was just a drop in the bucket.
  - This is the best thing since sliced bread.
  - You're a feast for sore eyes.
  - The boy grew like a weed.
  - Her great-grandmother was as old as the hills.
  - Don't bite off more than you can chew.
  - I am shaking like a leaf.
  - After his second suspension, he was walking on thin ice.
  - Her chest was as flat as a pancake.
  - Leave no stone unturned.

- Write a poem that is comprised entirely of "tell" statements that make clear statements about a topic.

  - Rewrite the "tell" poem, replacing each statement with images that bring the statement to life.
  - Revise the poem a third time, using a mix of the original "tell" statements with "show" imagery.

❦ 5 ❧
EXCAVATE YOUR MIND MINE: FREEWRITING

At one time or another, we all find ourselves thinking the same thoughts over and over again. The more we think them, the less fresh and interesting these thoughts become. This can dull our poetry blades significantly. When you want to leave the well-traveled path of your routine thinking for the adventure of an unknown destination, freewriting can take you there.

Freewriting is a way of training yourself to receive and transmit fresh ideas automatically. Just as your body knows how to breathe without conscious effort, your mind knows how to channel inspiration without you thinking about it. But first you may need to break some bad habits that interfere with your ability to send and receive. The goal of freewriting is to move from conscious, deliberate writing to automatic, subconscious writing. Freewriting can liberate you from ideas of who you are supposed to be on the page and what your writing is supposed to accomplish.

The mechanics of freewriting are simple: Choose a time limit, put your pen to the page or your hands on the keyboard, and don't stop until your time is up. You can start with any thought or phrase. Don't try too hard to choose your subject matter; it will choose you. And don't worry about the quality of what you're writing. The most important thing is to keep going, even if you have to write the same sentence over and over again until something new arrives.

As the rhythm of a train can rock you to sleep, the rhythm of your writing can lull your conscious mind into silence. Staying in motion creates a physical momentum that releases you from your habits of judging your writing and your ideas, thus giving you access to the raw, buried treasures of your mind. At its best, freewriting gives you yourself, unedited. You gain visibility into the themes, words, colors, and stories that pool up at the back of your mind as they spill forth onto the page.

Think of freewriting as a lightning rod attuning you to the currents coming through. And be careful not to confuse this practice with journal writing. Journals are for recording and examining your thoughts, feelings, and experiences; the goal of freewriting is to sidestep self-conscious self-scrutiny to find what is most alive in your mind.

TRY THIS!

- Set a timer for ten minutes. Put your pen to paper or your fingers to keyboard. Write without stopping until the buzzer sounds. Every time you get stuck, simply repeat whatever you last wrote until something new comes. Have patience with yourself. This may not be as easy as it sounds.

  When you finish, close the notebook or document. Do not look back over what you have written. It's important that you not judge your writing as being good or bad. Just let it be and move on.

  The next day, take a look at what you've written. Think of yourself as an archeologist looking for treasure rather than an editor seeking problems to fix. If you see any words, phrases, or ideas that are surprising or interesting to you, highlight them.

- You may want to create a separate document, notebook, or file where you collect all of your favorite freewriting discoveries in one place. You can add to the list with each freewriting you do.

- Set some type of cumulative goal for yourself. Try freewriting for ten minutes every day for a week. After you accomplish that goal, maybe you're ready to stretch your freewriting time to fifteen minutes per sitting, then twenty. What if you were to freewrite every day for a month?

- Notice what happens with your writing over time. Do you see any patterns or themes in your writing? Are you getting looser? Is the writing coming more easily? How is your relationship to writing changing the more your freewriting practice develops?

- Consider how you'd like to use freewriting. I use freewriting the way some people use a dry martini—to transition from the workday and relax into a different state of mind. I generally start every poetry-writing session with a quick freewrite to get the ideas flowing. How will you use freewriting in your writing practice? It's okay if you don't know, or if the use changes over time. That's the beauty of this practice—it's yours to play with however you'd like. It will evolve as you do.

 ## An Example From My Freewriting Archives

It is 10:30 and I am tired. The kittens have slowed down to a minor chord, draped over Sebastian's stuff half ornament, half forgotten from the other world where the melodies live. It is ugly the way the kittens strike the carpet, so angular and changing. I want to find myself open to memory, want to find a rhythm, to seek the strange chords, and let the feeling of the cats moving lift me, with my head turned up towards where the idea of heaven lives. I love to align myself with the wall, because in theory things line up then, all open like the buttons of my jeans, and the way that the truth filters in between the blinds like light. I know so much with just my fingers. The melody slides behind, like the child who everyone forgets. Keeping everyone connected. I take the wood table and leave it behind. There are beginners and people who don't try. Taking the first step, I find the force to be more solid than meaningful.

ᦔ 6 ᦔ
POETIC PHEROMONES:
ATTRACTING YOUR TRUE SUBJECTS

Fear of the blank page can keep many a poet from sitting down, rolling up her sleeves, and getting started. It's quite common for poets to get stuck wondering what they might have to say that's worthy of a poem. You may not know how many ideas you already have flowing through you and how much raw material of emotion, story, and language are waiting at the tip of your pen or fingertips until you start writing them down.

Following is a list of questions and prompts that can help you start exploring the subjects that are most magnetic for you. You may be surprised by the subject list that emerges. It can be tempting to write off certain topics as not worthy of poetry. We all want to write what we believe would most impress somebody out there: our mother, our rabbi, our garbage collector, our poet peers.

However, the truth is that it doesn't matter much what we want to write. More often than not, rather than choosing our subjects or themes, we are chosen by our poems. This can be very uncomfortable. I remember my cheeks burning with humiliation years ago when I was introduced at a reading at Cody's Books in Berkeley, California, as a poet "who writes about love." At that time in my life, I wanted only to write about social justice, history, mysticism—subjects that I decided had far more value than what I was actually called to write.

When I discovered Sharon Olds, a poet of great importance to me whose books focus primarily on the intimacies and bitter truths of family life, it occurred to me what a loss it would be for me and poetry readers around the world if this poet had decided that her somewhat unprecedented subject matter was not worthy. This completely changed my relationship with my own poems; I made a commitment to write about whatever moved me, no matter how illegitimate it might seem to me.

As I turned my attention away from what I thought I was supposed to be writing and toward what I felt called to write, my poetry took on new momentum. I felt more confidence in myself and my work. I hope you will make a similar choice. The best poems are the ones that demand to be written.

Answer these questions about yourself:

- What types of books and magazines are on your shelves?

- What do you do when you have a day or a night of free time?

- What classes do you take, or would you take, if you could?

- Where do you like to vacation, and what do you do there?

- Who have you not forgiven?

- What are the recurring themes in your dreams?

- What did you dream about last night?

- What is most embarrassing or impressive about your family? What story would they never forgive you for telling?

- What is your ethnicity, race, religion, spirituality?

- What challenges have you faced in life?

- What are you most passionate about?

- What did someone tell you about yourself in elementary school that you still believe?

- What's the one mistake you swore you would never admit to anyone?

- What memories haunt you?

- What book do you wish you'd written yourself?

- Which celebrity or movie character do you most resemble—in appearance, philosophy, or approach to life?

- What information do you retain flawlessly and effortlessly?

- What time period in history most intrigues you?

- Which of the Seven Dwarfs would you be?

- Which neighborhood, city, state, or country is most significant to you? Which would you most like to explore right now?

- If you were a dog, what breed might you be?

- What illness or malady scares you the most?

- What topics do your friends come to you for advice about?

- Did you have a special hideout or safe place as a child? What was it like? Why did you go there?

- What type of natural scenery most moves you?

- What foods do you love or hate to cook or eat?

- What do you believe about love?

- What do you want to understand about love?

- What topic do you know inside and out?

- What makes you laugh the loudest?

- What color makes you cringe?

- What texture makes you want to curl up inside it and take a luxurious nap?

- Which element are you most drawn to: earth, water, metal, wood, or fire?

- How do you like your eggs?

- Who are your heroes?

- What is your most vivid childhood memory?

- Who do you want to be when you grow up?

Because your relationship with the raw material of your life will evolve over time, return to these questions as often as you need to.

THIRTEEN WAYS OF LOOKING

Wallace Stevens' famous poem "Thirteen Ways of Looking at a Blackbird" includes thirteen numbered stanzas, each portraying the blackbird in a different light. I think of this as a poem not only about blackbirds but also about poetry. Writing poetry is about discovering ways of looking. It gives us the opportunity to slow down and really pay attention. As you practice looking and practice writing that is informed by looking, you may start to notice some patterns about the ways you look, or the things you look for.

While studying a blackbird, for example, you may uncover your own thirst for flight or your biases about the color black. You may look up and discover the strange shape of buildings and trees against the sky. Or maybe the blackbird rearranging its wings reminds you of your grandfather coming in from the cold, shaking snow from his long black overcoat. My point is that in considering the blackbird carefully, you tap into your own cosmology for "blackbird" and start seeing, imagining, and thinking about all kinds of things that are in some way related.

A poem that begins with the study of a blackbird could end up having nothing to do with blackbirds at all. Instead, a poet might engage with the grandfather image, and go on to write a poem about the lineage of men in his family. In this way, looking becomes a kind of portal when writing poetry. The subject or object you are studying is more likely to become the point of entry than the definitive end point of the poem.

THIRTEEN WAYS OF LOOKING

Any time you approach a subject and get stuck about how or what to write about it, consider these thirteen ways of looking:

1. Study the physical characteristics of your subject or object. Consider all that apply: its shape, size, color, texture, smell, taste, weight, heft, and sound.

2. If it moves, how does it move? In what directions? At what speed? Using what energy source? Toward or away from what? If it doesn't move, describe the quality of its stillness.

3. What was this thing or being made to do? How does it do this? Using what skills and parts?

4. When was the last time you encountered such a thing or being? What were you doing and thinking then? How does this experience compare to your previous experience? If this is your first experience with your subject, is there an interesting story about why you've waited until now, or what led you here?

5. Describe the context of this thing or being you are observing. Is it in a zoo, in your sock drawer, or straddling a fence? What do you notice about its surroundings? What do they look like, feel like, sound like? How does your subject seem to belong—or not—in this space?

6. What does your subject remind you of? Think of all the senses, not just the obvious ones. What does it look like, smell like, sound like, taste like, move like? Are there objects that are similar to this? Does your subject remind you of people (either ones you know intimately, or historical, literary, or mythical figures)?

7. What about this thing or being resembles you? Think along the lines of shape, size, color, behavior, habitat, personality, lifestyle, and features. What about it is the opposite of you?

8. Why did you choose this object or person to study? What about it or her appeals to you or repulses you?

9. If you were this object or person, what would you do or think and why?

10. Imagine this thing or being in a context that is completely alien to it (such as a blackbird in your sock drawer). How did it get there? How is it behaving and feeling in this context?

11. Pretend you are the predator of this being (the hawk that eats the blackbird) or purchaser of this object. Describe your relationship to it.

12. What kind of memories might your subject or object have accumulated? Who and what does it celebrate? Does it seek revenge? Forgiveness?

13. What about your subject or object most inspires and excites you? Why did you choose to study it?

～ 8 ～
TALK YOUR WALK: WORD CHOICE

"I love the word 'abide.' I tell myself, 'Wait,'
but it's not the same. 'Be patient' is more
burdensome and implies some kind of payoff.
'Endure' seems coarse and painful; 'abide'
seems peaceful and accepting."

—Lane Browning

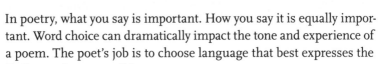

In poetry, what you say is important. How you say it is equally important. Word choice can dramatically impact the tone and experience of a poem. The poet's job is to choose language that best expresses the feeling and context of the poem.

For example, you might choose "endure" to describe a cancer patient making it through a rough day, and use "wait" to describe someone stopped at a traffic light. "Abide" feels a bit formal to me, and with a flair of romance. I picture a young man at the feed shop a century ago. He knows instantly that he loves the young woman at the cash register, goes home to change into his Sunday suit, and returns to the store to propose marriage to her. As the woman blushes and fumbles in surprise, the man abides, awaiting an answer. What does "abide" conjure for you?

SOME THINGS TO CONSIDER
When selecting language in a poem, you may want to ask yourself:

- Where and in what time period is the poem set? How do people speak? Are there any cultural or geographical influences on the way language is used there? Local slang, lingo, or colloquialisms? (Language spoken on the street in L.A. in the 1980s is different than that used in a Victorian parlor.)

- What is the natural world doing? Are there seasonal, lighting, or weather influences on the poem that affect its language? (How might smog words differ from thunderstorm words? What language would sunrise conjure compared to sunset?)

- What is the emotional tone of the poem? Is it angry? Peaceful? Excited? Remorseful?

- What happens in the poem, and how might language best buoy this action?

Using language that is typically associated with a certain place, time, or emotion can viscerally evoke a subject or theme. Other times, predictably appropriate language can feel uninspired or clichéd. In this case, it could be interesting to play against expectations by finding surprising language that is out of sync with the typical associations. The best way to find the language that will be most successful in any poem is to experiment, and then experiment some more.

Which approach did Ron Koertge took in "Cinderella's Diary"?

CINDERELLA'S DIARY | BY RON KOERTGE

I miss my stepmother. What a thing to say
but it's true. The prince is so boring: four
hours to dress and then the cheering throngs.
Again. The page who holds the door is cute
enough to eat. Where is he once Mr. Charming
kisses my forehead goodnight?

Every morning I gaze out a casement window
at the hunters, dark men with blood on their
boots who joke and mount, their black trousers
straining, rough beards, callused hands, selfish,
abrupt . . .

Oh, dear diary—I am lost in ever after:
Those insufferable birds, someone in every
room with a lute, the queen calling me to look
at another painting of her son, this time
holding the transparent slipper I wish
I'd never seen.

TRY THIS!

- Make a list of five different words each for:

  - happy
  - place of residence
  - forward motion
  - surprised
  - scared
  - rain

  Describe in a situation where you'd use each of the words. For example:

  - surprised

    » shocked: He found out as an adult that he was adopted.
    » startled: The teacher slams a book down on my desk as I'm dozing off.
    » blindsided: She discovers her husband is having an affair with the nanny.

- Choose a situation from your list above. Write a poem bringing it to life. Let's say you choose "Found out as an adult that he was adopted." In this poem, use one of the words you listed for happy, place of residence, forward motion, surprised, scared, and rain—the one that is the best fit for this context.

- Find three words in your poem that could be replaced with synonyms that are a better fit for the spirit, time, place, atmosphere, and narrative of this poem. Refer to "Some Things to Consider" on pages 28 and 29 to explore your options.

- Write a poem that uses all of these words and phrases, each expressing a different shade of meaning:

  - wait
  - be still
  - be patient
  - endure
  - abide

- As Ron Koertge did, choose a classic fairy tale and write a poem about what happens next, after the fairy tale ends. Write in the voice of the hero or heroine, as if they were living in your neighborhood today.

- Write a poem that vividly describes an event using language specific to that experience. (Let's say you start with a ballet in New York City, as described by a typical adult ballet patron.) Revise the poem to share the same experience, but use language that would be completely unexpected. (For example, how would a bullfighter in Spain describe this ballet, or a logger, or a small child?)

༡ 9 ༢

LIVING THE LIFE POETIC

"When you approach even the simplest object,
the depth that you see in that object will be
proportionate to the depth you bring to it."

—John O'Donohue

The Indian sitar includes both strings that are plucked and strings that are not. The strings not played directly are called sympathetic strings. These resonate with and echo harmonically the strings that have been plucked. I see the sitar as an apt metaphor for the poet. Everyone has strings that we pluck directly in order to make things happen and interact with people in our day-to-day lives. But poets are also equipped with sympathetic strings of rumination that resonate with a kind of kindred music in response to the events, ideas, people, and experiences that impact us. Writing poetry moves naturally from this call and response. In effect, living poetically leads to writing poetically.

So, how does one live the life poetic? This kind of receptivity takes practice, especially in this fast-paced world where it is more common and acceptable to exhaust ourselves doing things rather than slowing down to digest those experiences that move us.

Years ago when my dog Henry was a puppy and we lived in San Francisco, he taught me an important lesson about tuning into the marvels of the mundane. On our morning constitutional through Golden Gate Park, we encountered an empty chips bag lying in the grass along the gravel path. As Henry noticed the crumpled red, metallic paper riffling in the wind, the hair on his back and neck went up. I thought: Doritos. Henry thought: Mysterious Unknown. He

32   WRITING THE LIFE POETIC

carefully approached the object, took a cautious sniff, and then leapt back and barked, awaiting the bag's next move.

In this moment, Henry reminded me that I have an opportunity to be surprised, moved, and changed by the endless unexpected variables that emerge in familiar routines. I believe that this is what poetry demands of us: a willingness to savor mystery instead of stampeding toward certainty. When we pay careful attention to the potential of the extraordinary, its blossoms will burst through our ordinary, everyday lives.

Following are some ideas that can help you develop a practice of receptivity and attune yourself to the poetry you are already living.

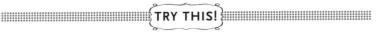

TRY THIS!

- Leave your house, apartment, yurt, dormitory, or office and spend an hour out in the world observing. Whether you're sitting on a bench in a deserted park or jostling through Grand Central Station, your only job is to look, listen, and notice what catches your attention. Come home and write a description of one sight you saw, one sound you heard, one memory that was evoked, and one discovery you made. This exercise will get easier the more you practice it.

- Write a poem through the eyes of a child or young animal. Imagine that she is having her first significant experience of some kind: tasting sugar, discovering toilet water. Explore the marvels of this moment in language and imagery.

- Every day for a week, pay close attention to a routine that you complete on autopilot: brushing your teeth, chopping onions, driving carpool to chess club. Really study the sounds, smells, thoughts, feelings, physical motion, and surrounding environment of this experience as if you've never had it before. Then consider the beliefs that have shaped each of those routines: cavities are painful and expensive; home-cooked meals are healthy; I want my children to grow up to be brilliant strategists. At the end of the week, write down as many details about your routine as you can remember, and describe what you've discovered through studying it.

- Go someplace you go regularly—work, a café, a library—and pretend you've never been there before. Study everything and everyone around you as if you were a detective looking for clues. Write down every single detail you never noticed before: Susan's left ear has four piercings, while her right ear only has one; the floor is linoleum with a gray and white swirl pattern; the smell of ground coffee makes you think of death.

- Return in your mind to someplace you've lived. Without actually describing the place itself, describe the sights, sounds, and associations that are your mental and visceral references for this place. For example, what did the light look like slanting across the balcony at sunset? How did the faint sounds of children playing in the schoolyard get baked into your pancakes? Remember how surprised you were to realize that garbage trucks in New York City make their rounds at two A.M.?

∽ 10 ∽
DO WHAT YOU KNOW: TRANSLATE ANOTHER CREATIVE PROCESS TO POETRY

"My commercial graphics are based on words: I begin with lists of noteworthy qualities that define a client's unique identity, then I translate this information into a concise graphic representation. A financial enterprise with all its roots and branches, employees and clients, products and services, becomes, say, a red key. The endeavor is to boil a broad message down to its simplest and quickest evocation. With poetry I reverse the transformative course: starting with almost nothing–a detail–I seek to blow up the particular into the universal, to draw out the whole from a minute part. The distant barking of a dog, dishes drying on a rack, a drop of wine, any of these things–if lit with the proper fuse–can be propelled skyward and carry me along."

—Grégoire Vion

Many people come to poetry thinking that they don't know the first thing about it. What they don't realize is how the creative processes they're already using—from sorting the mail to solving problems at work to creating the family dinner menu—are readily transferable to writing poetry. Maybe you have come to poetry from the launching pad of another creative hobby or passion—such as scrapbooking, taking photographs, or playing the drums. A good way into poetry is to start with the skills you've been cultivating in your creativity arsenal. You may be surprised how well they translate to poetry.

For example, I recently had a student insist that she couldn't write poetry because she didn't understand how to write images. Shortly thereafter, she started playing with words, and she discovered that she had a good feel for the sound and rhythm of language as a result of her experience making musical arrangements. Through flexing creative muscles that were already strong, she wrote a poem that sounded terrific; she even surprised herself by writing several unexpectedly fine images.

My friend Pam crafts collages of various found objects and materials, using texture, color, and composition to tell visual stories. The day that she cut text phrases out of an old book and arranged them as part of her composition, Pam created her first "found poem." This was a very natural way into the world of poetry for her. (You'll learn all about found poems in chapter twenty-one.)

I came to poetry from visual art, a practice that trained me in the art of observation. From drawing and painting, I had learned to discern the shape of things in relationship to each other through comparison and contrast. This prepared me well to see similarities in seemingly unlike things, such as pigeons and raisins:

> Pigeons fumbling on ledges
> like raisins in bread.
> Dark sweet spots of pity.

(an excerpt from "Oratorio")

Probably the most important thing my art training taught me was patience. It took me years to be able to look at something and really capture it on canvas in a way that satisfied me. Therefore, when I started writing poetry, I didn't expect to go out into the world and have pigeons and raisins falling out of trees into neat little similes. I had learned the hard (but fun) way that perception is a discipline that takes time and practice.

Some of us are more visual, others more auditory. You may bring to writing an innate sense of timing or rhythm. Or maybe you are a magnet for interesting dialects—or a person to whom everyone always tells their darkest secrets. Whatever delights or inspires you most . . . whatever is the most natural way for you to think creatively is your launching pad for writing poems. Start where you are. It is your unique way into a life of poetry.

- What are you really good at? Reading maps? Solving cross-word puzzles? Entertaining your cat? Make a comprehensive list of all the things you know how to do well. Don't worry about being grandiose: Cooking a stir fry, tying a shoe, and talking on the phone can all be on the list if they apply. Creative talents are good, but you'll want to stretch your definition of this, too. If you're great at negotiating for the best salary or convincing your kids to come home by their curfew, these are also creative talents.

- Choose a talent or skill from this list and write an instructional poem that shares your know-how with others. For example, a poem title might be "How to Make a Spring Salad From Your Garden," or, "The Art of the Double-Knot."

- Choose an area of expertise from the list and write a poem that employs the same techniques or thought processes you use to excel in this area. If you chose cooking, for example, and you're good at cooking because of the way you blend colors, textures, and fragrances, experiment with how this skill can translate to writing a poem.

IN THE MOUTH OF THE BEHOLDER | BY GRÉGOIRE VION

With Gunpowder leaves in water,
untwisting as if for the end of winter
you may be drawn
to further things in China,
the Iron Goddess of Compassion, jade.
On the other hand,

Lipton Brisk you can use
to draw a horse in a rusty coat,
or sip in Ireland with milk,
and chubby beans on toast,
in the house of a house painter
dedicated to yellow.

᭡ 11 ᭡
COME TO YOUR SENSES

"I think that one role of the poet is to present the
reader/listener with his or her view of what the
world could be, in contrast with how it is."

—Christopher Luna

Everyone knows that fire is hot and ice is cold; we cry when we're sad and smile when we're happy. But it may be less obvious how happy tastes, how sad smells, or what hot sounds like? How does cold dress? When we let go of the standard sensory and emotional associations and instead juxtapose them in unexpected combinations, we can discover new ways of seeing, perceiving, understanding, and communicating. This can serve a poem very well.

For example, in my poem "Bai Hua," about a child I sponsor in a Chinese orphanage, I could have written, "I empathize with Bai Hua, because I, too, have spent many years alone." Instead, I chose to write, "I know the metal taste of alone." This phrase conflates the sense of taste with metal—something not commonly tasted—and the emotion of loneliness to create an image that is a little surprising. I made this choice by feel: because the cold, unyielding nature of metal signifies "alone" to me. Because I think of eating as one of the primary social pleasures, I chose taste as the sense that registers loneliness.

The decisions I made in this example do not demonstrate any particular rule that should be repeated pro forma. I share them with you as a window into the type of exploration you can make as you consider which words belong together and why. Each person's individual sense of logic and intuition will bring to life an abstraction like "loneliness" in a unique way.

These types of juxtapositions are not natural for most people, and this is why they can be so rich. When you think in the same old patterns in which you've always thought, you're likely to churn out the same old words and images you've always written. By experimenting with ways to sidestep your ordinary phrasings, you may discover new approaches to emotionally difficult subject matter or you may reinvent clichés.

Think of mixing up emotions and senses as upending the snow globe of your mind. With a few vigorous shakes, you completely change the landscape!

TRY THIS!

- Poet Leanne Grabel invites her students of all ages to personify the inanimate, the emotional, and the visceral through interview questions such as the ones here. Answer each question quickly, as if you are in a game show and it's important to be faster than your competitor.

   - Who does red love?
   - What kind of shoes does anxiety wear?
   - What does jealousy eat for breakfast?
   - Where does fear live?
   - What did blue borrow, and why?
   - How does pink sing?
   - What does truth taste like?

- Write down a few paragraphs describing a particularly painful or embarrassing memory. Without ever naming how you felt, try to demonstrate the feelings through your use of description. Bring in as many unexpected senses as possible. For instance, what does shame sound like? How does regret taste? Where would one see forgiveness—or its shadow, revenge?

- Write an entire poem in which orange is the main character. What does orange want, do, feel, believe, remember? What happens to orange? What does orange learn?

- In what ways does the world mirror loneliness for you? In the freshly laundered scent of a snowdrift at dusk? In the droning eyes of Mona Lisa? In the thirst of water dripping from the tap? Make a list of ten descriptions of loneliness, each using different sensory detail.

Examples From Students of Leanne Grabel

Nervous tastes like ice, like meat,
like school lunches, carrots, water.

      —Vera Boylen (age 9)

Ocean Blue is the child of jeans and blueberries.
She smells like Scotch tape.

      —Javalah Makia (age 8)

Sadness smells like prunes and potions.
She sleeps on a cot.
Ego is her idol.

      —Kennedy McEntee (age 10)

Joy smells like roses, cheesy roses.
Eats blueberry pancakes.
Drinks root beer.
Loves a grilled cheese sandwich.

      —Margery Price (age 8)

༄ 12 ༄
WRITING TITLES

*"At best, the title is a source of light, illuminating
the poem's successive lines. At best, the sound of
the title echoes throughout the whole poem."*

—Paulann Petersen

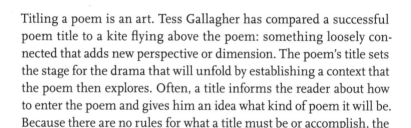

Titling a poem is an art. Tess Gallagher has compared a successful poem title to a kite flying above the poem: something loosely connected that adds new perspective or dimension. The poem's title sets the stage for the drama that will unfold by establishing a context that the poem then explores. Often, a title informs the reader about how to enter the poem and gives him an idea what kind of poem it will be. Because there are no rules for what a title must be or accomplish, the ways in which you write titles will be uniquely yours, In fact, some poems don't even have titles. Following are a few common approaches to titling that you may want to explore in your own work.

A poem's title can define a time period ("Civil War" by yours truly), a season ("Winter" by Marie Ponsot), or a moment in time ("The Day Lady Died" by Frank O'Hara). Or it may establish a specific location ("Cannon Beach At Sunset") or a general one ("Over the Mountain" by William Stafford). It can let the reader know whom the poem is about or name the extended metaphor that will be explored ("The Lanyard" by Billy Collins).

You can create a title at any time in the poem writing process. Sometimes the title may be your point of entry for a poem. Or you might not arrive at the "true" title until you've reached the end. While the poem is taking shape, I recommend thinking of any title you write as a placeholder. It's important not to commit to the title too early, as it may lock you into a trajectory that the poem does not ultimately want to travel.

Writing a poem can feel much like trying to steer a runaway car. You think you're headed to the supermarket, but then suddenly the poem gains momentum in some other direction, and you're heading at breakneck speed into that empty lot where Jason Phillips beat up your brother in second grade. As the journey of the poem unfolds, you may end up editing the supermarket entirely out of the final poem, making the title "Aisle Two, Bulk Cashews" completely irrelevant. Once the poem has revealed itself and is fully formed, that's the time to think about finalizing your title.

One positive outcome of choosing an ill-suited title early in the writing process is that it can become an itch that keeps you scratching until you've discovered more about what the poem truly wants to be. Sometimes the wrong title can lead you from what looks like a dead end through a porthole into some topic or theme you might not have otherwise discovered.

TRY THIS!

- Wendell Berry titled the poem below with a phrase excerpted from the poem (not shown here). If this were your poem, which phrase would you choose to be the poem's title? Select three different phrases that you think might work.

    When despair for the world grows in me
    and I wake in the night at the least sound
    in fear of what my life and my children's lives may be,
    I go and lie down where the wood drake
    rests in his beauty on the water, and the great heron
          feeds.
    I come into the peace of wild things
    who do not tax their lives with forethought
    of grief. I come into the presence of still water.
    And I feel above me the day-blind stars
    waiting with their light. For a time
    I rest in the grace of the world, and am free.

- Wondering how to title a poem? Not sure if the title you chose is working well? Ask yourself these questions to explore the range of possibilities available to you. Keep experimenting until you find the one that fits best:

  - Do I want the reader to know exactly what this poem will be about after reading the title? Do I want them to know who is speaking, or what time period is covered, or where the poem is set?

  - How would a more abstract title—one that represents a key theme of the poem—work? (An example is "The Weight" by Linda Gregg, a poem that intimately studies the relationship of two horses.)

  - Is there exposition in the poem that could be cut and replaced with a title? (The Chinese poet Tu Fu does this well in the poem "Alone, Looking for Blossoms Along the River.")

  - Would the first line work well as a title?

  - Would the last line work well as a title?

  - Is there a phrase within the poem that captures the essence of what the poem is about?

  - How can I use the title to shed light on or add depth to the poem?

FORGIVE AND FORGET: LETTING GO OF WHAT'S HOLDING BACK YOUR WRITING

When I was in the tenth grade, I wrote a paper exploring the themes of T.H. White's *The Once and Future King*. While crafting the conclusion, I stumbled upon a truth I had not previously understood about the book and about the human condition. This was my first glimpse of the revelations that await us on the other side of the labor of writing.

I proudly gave the paper to my father to read and stood beside him nervously as he did so. When he was finished, he paused, then shook his head slowly. This scared me. Maybe I had misjudged and it was a terrible paper after all. Then my father said with a quiet reverence, "My darling daughter, you are a writer." And I believed him. Today, I believe him, still.

I often marvel at how the words of even a casual acquaintance can influence our direction and ability to claim our lives. Words can carry us beyond the limitations of our self-image into an entirely new possibility. Or they can bring our dreams to a screeching halt of self-doubt.

What have you been told about your writing over the years? Was it positive? Negative? How has it influenced what you believe you are capable of today?

Take a moment to clean out the filing cabinet of your memory. Find a special place for those moments and people that remind you how fabulous you are, and get rid of the rest! This will give you more space for receiving the good news and positive feedback that await you.

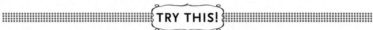

- Write a list of your own beliefs about your writing that you're ready to reinvent, then reinvent them, like so:

I used to believe	Now I believe
I used to believe other people's criticism about my writing.	Now I believe in my own capacity to evaluate my writing.
I used to believe that I do not write images well.	Now, after reading chapters four and nineteen and doing the exercises, I believe that I can write surprising, interesting images.
I used to believe that poetry was too difficult to write.	Now I believe that poetry is not only possible, but fun.
I used to believe that I don't understand poetry.	After reading chapter thirty-seven, now I believe that not all poems are meant to be literally understood, and that there are more ways to appreciate poetry than making sense of the narrative.

- Write down the most positive thing you've been told about your writing. Then write down the most negative thing you've been told. Write a few sentences describing the people who told you these things, and the context in which you were given this feedback. Then take the mirror of other people's opinions and put them to your own creative use. Write a poem in which both the most positive and most negative statements appear.

- Rainer Maria Rilke's *Letters to a Young Poet* makes public ten letters of encouragement that the poet wrote to a young student, with wisdom such as:

> Go into yourself and test the deeps in which
> your life takes rise; at its source you will
> find the answer to the question whether
> you must create. Accept it, just as it sounds,
> without inquiring into it. Perhaps it will
> turn out that you are called to be an artist.
> Then take that destiny upon yourself and
> bear it, its burden and its greatness, with-
> out ever asking what recompense might
> come from outside.

What advice do you wish you had received to inform your own poetry writing? What advice do you wish to pass onto others who may have been discouraged or deterred along the way? Write a poem titled, "Letter to a Young Poet," in which you invite yourself and others into the realm of poetry and offer the permission you feel is most needed to inhabit this realm with freedom and delight.

TRUTH, LIES, AND PERSONAL SPACE

*"No, these stories are not true, but they are the
truth of what I'm working on now. The truth of
what I want to capture and hold in my hands
just long enough to bring it to life and then let
it go. Truth? Lies? Or a little of both, woven
together to become even more true. Perhaps
that's my true job as a writer ... not to tell
truth, but to create it."*

—Shanna Germain

At an open mic reading in San Francisco, back when I was in my
early twenties, I bumped into a woman who was an old friend of my
boyfriend. When I got up to read a poem that was about a somewhat
cavalier sexual experience, I could feel the woman's eyes boring into
me as I read. At the end of the reading, she and her twin sister cor-
nered me in the small press section of the bookstore and demanded to
know what happened next—in the real-life postscript to the poem.

This unacceptable behavior reflects two common mistakes made
by uninitiated poetry readers.

Mistake no. 1: They presume the "I" of the poem is the poet, and
that the poem is about an experience that the poet actually had. This
may or may not be true. The truth is, in poetry there is no real truth.
There is only the poem. Even if it is excerpted from an actual experience, the poem becomes something somewhat beyond "true" as
it is sculpted by music, imagery, rhythm, and line into something
representative of itself.

Poets write about all kinds of experiences that may more figura-
tively than literally reflect what actually happened to them. I have a

friend who is happily married, yet writes poems exploring failed marriages. I wrote a poem that begins, "Our dead son talks around us," but I do not literally have a dead son. The poem is a space where you don't have to be strictly yourself. You can try on any number of other lives to explore something you want to better understand, or you can inhabit your own shadow in a way that you would never dare in real life.

When you read poetry, do not expect poems to report journalistically on life experience. The rules of engagement for reading poetry are that the poem is fair game for discussion, but the poet's life is not. When speaking about a poem, the appropriate way to reference the "I" of a poem is as "the speaker." It is important to follow this decorum when you participate in a poetry-writing workshop or a discussion group, or when you have an opportunity to speak to a poet directly about her work.

Mistake no. 2: Readers experience the poem as an open door into a poet's personal space, where they believe they have been invited in to snoop around. This, simply, is bad manners. If a dinner guest were to get up at the end of a meal and rummage through the cupboards to see what else there was to eat, the host would rightfully be offended. Likewise it is not polite for the reader to ask for more than she has been given when listening to poetry. The poem is the public offering drawn from the poet's private life or imagination. There are no visiting privileges. End of story.

As a writer of poetry, being off the hook about literal truth is good news. You have more room to play around with a scene or narrative or image if you feel free to use it not just literally but also symbolically—to explore overarching emotional truths, in addition to specific personal-experience truths. You can also boldly, blatantly make stuff up in poems. I'd like to see someone corner Jay Leeming after hearing him read this poem, and ask him what happened next!

I Pick Up a Hitchhiker | by Jay Leeming

After a few miles, he tells me
that my car has no engine.
I pull over, and we both get out
and look under the hood.
He's right.
We don't say anything more about it
all the way to California.

- Play the game Two Truths and a Lie in a poem. Tell a story in which two events or facts or moments are true, and one is invented.

- Write a poem in which the speaker has the most humiliating, embarrassing experience you could possibly imagine: something you'd never dream of doing. Notice how you draw from the well of your own personal experience to explore and convey the emotion of the experience even though you're describing an experience that you did not actually have.

- Write a poem in which something that could not literally happen happens, just as Jay Leeming's speaker drives to California without an engine.

ᘜ 15 ᘚ
POINT OF VIEW:
THE POWER OF PRONOUNS

Point of view is an instrument of intimacy: it orchestrates the reader's distance from (or proximity to) the speaker. Your first instinct may be to recount your own personal experiences using the first-person, singular point of view—the *I*. This is a fine approach that can serve a poem well. However, because this is often the most obvious and natural way to go, I recommend experimenting with other point-of-view options to get a feel for how they might benefit a poem.

When you replace *I* with *you* in a poem (known as second person), you invite the reader to participate in a new way. *You* can be read different ways; it can mean "one"—a general, universal point of view—or it can literally mean "you," thus including the reader in the action of the poem. *You* can also be a direct address to someone specific: "You left me; how could you?" In this case, the reader may be positioned as an eavesdropper overhearing words directed at someone else—or they may find themselves standing in for that person.

What happens when a first-person experience is transferred to the third person (*he/she*)? The advantage of the third person is that it gives both the poet and the reader some personal space from the action of the poem. They observe rather than participate. This can create breathing room to write things you might not otherwise feel comfortable expressing. For example, consider "He wanted to die" versus "I want to die." The first person feels immediate and urgent. The third person feels less immediate; we read it less personally.

Experiment with pronouns to help you find the point of view that best expresses what you want to say while making the depth of connection you want.

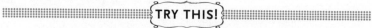

- Take a published poem you admire and rewrite it in two different points of view. Observe how the different pronouns change the experience of the poem.

- Write a poem about a life-changing moment in your life. Instead of *I*, use *he* or *she*. How does it feel to write as if this experience happened to someone else?

- Write a poem that speaks directly to someone important to you about an experience that you have shared. Imagine there is no reader beyond this person. Then rewrite the poem as if you are describing the same experience for a general audience. Which pronouns do you choose, and why? How do they serve each version of the poem?

౧౬ ౨
FAMILY FODDER

What do you know better than your own family? Who have you studied more closely? Who has traumatized you more successfully and tended to your needs with more ardor? We all depart from childhood with a vast archive of experience embossed on us like our own fingerprints. If you never left your house again, you'd have enough accumulated memories about your relationships and experiences from growing up to fuel a lifetime of poems. Tap the well of the past and see what poems await you there.

TRY THIS!

- Is there a legendary story that gets retold when the family gathers? Does each family member remember and tell it a little differently? Write this story from your point of view. Then from your mother's perspective. Next, from a sibling's perspective. What did the dog think?

- What has a parent or other elder in your family taught you that still resonates today? With Don Colburn's poem "Wildflowers" on page 55 as your example, explore what is meaningful and memorable about this lesson. What does it reveal about you and the person from whom you learned it?

- Write a poem in which you expose a family secret that could get you in trouble—or has already gotten you in trouble. (Keep in mind that I'm not necessarily advocating publishing it ...

just writing it! There is often a lot of metaphoric momentum in stories that have been forbidden.)

- Write a poem about a room in your house or a special hiding place in your yard or neighborhood when you were a child. What happened there? What did it mean to you? How did your relationship with this place influence the person you are today? What would you do if you could go back there?

- Write a poem about something a family member did that you haven't forgiven. As Sharon Olds does in "The Elder Sister," on page 57 see if there's a moment of grace or gratitude that can give ballast to the painful memory.

- Now rewrite your poem from the perspective of the person you have not forgiven. Why might he have made the choices he made? What grudges might she still be holding against you?

- Describe a garment, toy, or other object that was of special significance to you in your childhood. Who gave it to you? What attracted you most to it? What did it mean to you then? What does it represent to you now?

- Paint a visual picture of a particular moment in time that conveys a larger family dynamic, as Rebecca McClanahan does in "Watching my Parents Sleeping Beside an Open Window Near the Sea" on page 56.

WILDFLOWERS | by Don Colburn

Until I heard the names in my own voice
I never saw them whole: chickweed, toothwort,
May apple, Dutchman's breeches, Indian pipe.
A list was my father's way of witnessing;
it made a flower real. And this afternoon
in the weedy meadow by the towpath,
I'm jotting odd names on a scrap of paper
for no one in particular, myself maybe
or my father. Back then I let him teach me
to look down at the ground for stars,
bells, shades of blue. He was never happier
than when we looked up accuracy's myriad names
and he wrote them out in slanted letters.
Now, over and over, like a child,
I say *gill-over-the-ground, gill-*
over-the-ground, gill-over-the-ground,
and in the saying see it blossom again
inside its spilled blue name.

Watching My Parents Sleeping Beside an Open Window Near the Sea | by Rebecca McClanahan

Needing them still, I come
when I can, this time to the sea
where we share a room: their double bed,
my single. Morning fog paints the pale
scene even paler. Lace curtains breathing,
the chenille spread folded back,
my father's feet white sails furled
at the edge of blue pajamas.
Every child's dream, a parent
in each hand, though this child is fifty.
Their bodies fit easily, with room
to spare. When did they grow
so small? *Grow* so small—
as if it were possible to swell
backwards into an earlier self.
On the bureau, their toys
and trinkets. His shaving brush
and pink heart pills, her gardenia
sachet. The tiny spindle that pricks
the daily bubble of blood, her sweet
chemistry. Above our heads
a smoke alarm pulses, its red eye beating.
One more year, I ask the silence.
Last night to launch myself
into sleep I counted their breaths, the tidal
rise and fall I now put my ear to,
the coiled shell of their lives.

THE ELDER SISTER | BY SHARON OLDS

When I look at my elder sister now
I think how she had to go first, down through the
birth canal, to force her way
head-first through the tiny channel,
the pressure of Mother's muscles on her brain,
the tight walls scraping her skin.
Her face is still narrow from it, the long
hollow cheeks of a Crusader on a tomb,
and her inky eyes have the look of someone who has
been in prison a long time and
knows they can send her back. I look at her
body and think how her breasts were the first to
rise, slowly, like swans on a pond.
By the time mine came along, they were just
two more birds in the flock, and when the hair
rose on the white mound of her flesh, like
threads of water out of the ground, it was the
first time, but when mine came
they knew about it. I used to think
only in terms of her harshness, sitting and
pissing on me in bed, but now I
see I had her before me always
like a shield. I look at her wrinkles, her clenched
jaws, her frown-lines—I see they are
the dents on my shield, the blows that did not reach me.
She protected me, not as a mother
protects a child, with love, but as a
hostage protects the one who makes her
escape as I made my escape, with my sister's
body held in front of me.

↳ 17 ↰

SEEING YOUR SELF IN
YOUR WORLD

I stopped to lean against a cement pillar as the wind
started picking up. It was a nice little private alcove,
protected by a Dumpster. I could see out into the
street, but I was not likely to be noticed. The street
was unusually quiet. There was a circle of fallen
leaves, as if the financial district were preparing
itself for winter. You don't see autumn leaves too
often in San Francisco, and I'm not sure how they
got there, among the twenty-story office buildings
and shopping centers. They must've blown in from
somewhere else. I pictured a wind lifting them from
my hometown on the east coast and carrying them
all the way here, as if they were some secret hinge
connecting my old life there to this one.

As the wind gathered momentum, like a bike
chain catching and propelling something large and
unlikely forward, the leaves spun up and started
circling. I told Jeff it was time for my teeth cleaning,
but it wasn't. I still had ten minutes. I hung up the
phone and stood there mesmerized as the leaves went
round and round in a perfect circle. They looked like
a halo that had lost its angel, lifted in the wind before
drifting down to the earth. I thought of the childhood game where you hold hands and spin very fast
chanting, "Ashes, ashes, we all fall down!"

Somehow, in that moment, my life changed. Those
leaves felt like a call and response. Something in
me was lifting, too, and falling. Circling fast, and
burning down. It was as if every choice I had ever
made was spinning in that circle. Thirty-three years
of small moments of questionable consequence
had strung themselves together into something
recognizable. A necklace of non-sequiturs. I sat
down right there on the pavement in my silk pants
and leather pumps. Indian style. I leaned against
the pole and put my head in my hands. Beside
me on the pavement, a mute phone. On the other
end, with his mute phone, Jeff, who was neither
interested in nor capable of love. Two blocks away,
a cubicle in a sea of cubicles, where I would spend
the rest of the day, the rest of the next three weeks,
the rest of my life, perhaps, failing to translate a
company's thirst for profit into some meaningful
message its customers could believe.

—Sage Cohen, from "Catharsis"

I include this excerpt from a personal essay as an example of how we
are constantly projecting ourselves onto the things around us. We see
things not as they are, but as we are. If you were to encounter that same
circle of leaves, or even if I were to see them a week or a month later,
we'd each have a completely different list of related memories and metaphors. What happens next in this essay is a hearty cry; you might have
laughed or cowered or shrugged your shoulders with indifference. Or,
you may have overlooked the leaves altogether in favor of the memories
triggered by the shape or color of the Dumpster in that alley, or the
name of the restaurant on the sandwich board across the street.

Seeing yourself in the things around you can give a poem a great
deal of energy. It can hone a vague scene into a potent moment of
emotional impact and meaning. When the reader knows why she is
being shown a circle of leaves and what it means to the speaker, she
can then sift through her own references and associations to find the

ones that connect with this moment. The paradox is that the more absolutely specific you are, the greater the chance of a universal appeal. Your moment, told with authenticity and precision, becomes everyone's moment. Put your heart, soul, memory, and emotional life into everything you study and every association you make, and your reader will follow you anywhere.

- Make a list of five pivotal moments or decisions in your life. Experiment with reliving each of these as an observer and writing down every sensory detail you can conjure from that moment in time. (What was the temperature of the ultrasound scope on your belly when the technician announced that you were having twins? How did your partner's pressure on your hand change? What was the pattern on the ceiling? How did the hum of the machine feel thrumming through your ribs? What did you see in the black-and-white exposure of the screen?) Chances are good that you have retained more information than you might think about experiences that have impacted you deeply. By writing, you may recapture insights and details that have otherwise been lost.

- Choose an image or sensory description from your list that feels the most powerful to you. Use that as the starting point or central metaphor for a poem.

- Without telling the actual story of what happened, write a poem that thoroughly explores the moment you selected with as much sensory description as possible.

- Notice how the images you have chosen are imbued with the thoughts, feelings, and discoveries that were triggered by this choice or experience—without actually reporting *about* them.

- Choose a name for the poem that represents the emotional truth of this moment.

ꙩ 18 ꙩ
FROM DYSFUNCTION TO DUENDE

"What is to give light must endure burning."

—Viktor Frankl

More often than not, when I tell people that I write poetry, they get a wistful, faraway look in their eyes. Exhaling deeply, they admit, "I used to write poetry once, too."

When I inquire as to why they no longer write poetry, the answer is so invariably the same that it's almost become a cliché: "I stopped writing because I got happy."

I admit I came to poetry on my knees, for the same reason so many of us do: because I had no idea how else I might survive. And this can be a powerful way to get initiated into the craft and life of poetry. However, contrary to cultural stereotypes, dysfunction doesn't make a poet, and poetry does not exist merely as a life support system to keep the dysfunctional groping along the bottom of things. Poetry at its best is a portal we write ourselves through, from the ecstasies of grief to the ecstasies of joy.

At a recent lecture, Elizabeth Gilbert observed that in the television show *Heroes*—where each character has a supernatural power—the artist character has a heroin addiction, the origin of which is never explained. In contrast, Gilbert pointed out, the cheerleader on the show does not require crystal meth to effectively shake her pom-poms. Why, she wondered, do we accept without question that the life of the artist demands this kind of self-destruction?

I think our artist/writer/poet mythology is born of a kind of romance with darkness that is sustained by the general public's avoidance of it. We look to our artists to live out the dark sides that many of us are not courageous enough to live ourselves. This is why, as a culture, and as writers, we often misunderstand the difference between duende and dysfunction: writing darkness versus living it.

I'm not saying that there are no poets who live darkness. Certainly, they're out there; Sylvia Plath, Anne Sexton, and John Berryman are some of the most famous poets who never emerged from their pain and ultimately ended their own lives. Many of us inhabit darkness and write our way out of it from time to time. But I think it does a disservice to poetry and to poets to romanticize or give credence to the idea that poetry is born and bred entirely of this dark place.

I remember as a young woman worrying about what I would write if I ever got happy. When I discovered the concept of "duende" in poet Federico García Lorca's essay "Theory and Play of the Duende," I was grateful to have a poetic reference for the complexity of exploring darkness through language. In this piece, García Lorca described duende as dark and potentially dangerous energy an artist is seeking to channel from within—a spirit of art at the other end of the spectrum from the Muse or Angel. (See page 63 excerpt from this essay.)

Duende is available to us when we call upon the wisdom of the wound or struggle—our own or that of the universal human experience—and use it to know ourselves more completely. When a poet taps into duende in his poetry, he becomes the conductive wire through which it moves, not the well in which darkness collects.

Much of my poetry is dark. People who know me well read it and have a difficult time reconciling their experience of my sunny disposition and my cloudy poems. For me, duende is the clarifying fire that burns through observation to spark the illumination of truth. Whether I'm happy or I'm sad, the mining of what is true can go deep into the darkness. When I emerge squinting into the light with the glorious gem of a word that fits just right, this is the ecstasy of poetry.

TRY THIS!

- Do you have a self-destructive habit? (It doesn't have to be life threatening; nail biting, staying up too late, or eating too much ice cream could qualify!) Write a poem that explores this habit's significance to you. Go deep into its pleasures and pains. Explore every facet of what draws you to this habit and keeps you there.

- Chiaroscuro is an Italian term that describes how the relationship between light and shadow defines a shape and gives it depth. In the spirit of chiaroscuro, write a poem about an experience so painful that it set you out to sea emotionally. Write about the return to joy (or peace) when you washed up on shore. Or, if you haven't arrived on the shore yet, write about what you'd imagine that experience to be.

- What wisdom does your shadow hold? What can it teach you? Write a poem in which you invite your shadow to take center stage and tell its story.

- Write a poem in which something good happens—in which the speaker feels pleased, moved, or satisfied. Avoid explanations of how the speaker feels. Let the emotional tenor resonate through the description of the experience.

An Excerpt From Federico García Lorca's essay "Theory and Play of the Duende"

"When the angel sees death appear he flies in slow circles, and with tears of ice and narcissi weaves the elegy we see trembling in the hands of Keats, Villasandino, Herrera, Bécquer, and Juan Ramón Jiménez. But how it horrifies the angel if he feels a spider, however tiny, on his tender rosy foot!

The duende, by contrast, won't appear if he can't see the possibility of death, if he doesn't know he can haunt death's house, if he's not certain to shake those branches we all carry, that do not bring, can never bring, consolation.

With idea, sound, gesture, the duende delights in struggling freely with the creator on the edge of the pit. Angel and Muse flee, with violin and compasses, and the duende wounds, and in trying to heal that wound that never heals, lies the strangeness, the inventiveness of a man's work."

ᴥ 19 ᴥ

FIGURATIVE IMAGES: METAPHOR MIRRORS AND SIMILE SEMBLANCES

In chapter four, we experimented with showing versus telling. Remember that "showing" involves using an image to convey information, and may include a literal image ("the black dog curled up on his red bed") or a figurative one ("the black dog curled tight as a fist"). Metaphors and similes are figurative images. In this chapter, we're going to consider how they can give new meaning or energy to your poetry and when to use each.

A *simile* puts together two unlike things and points out the similarities: "Her eyes were like diamonds." A *metaphor* says one thing equals another thing, thereby conflating and transforming two unlike things into something entirely new: "Her eyes were diamonds." Because metaphor is more declarative, redefining our known reality and expectations in the space of a few words, it typically makes a stronger statement. Let's take a look at a few examples from poems.

SIMILES

Example 1:

> My friend says she is like an empty drawer
> being pulled out of the earth
>
> (from "Little America" by Jason Shinder)

Chances are good that you have never thought to describe a feeling of loss, depression, or emptiness exactly this way before. Shinder gives us a new image here to add to our figurative repertoire. Who knows—maybe someday you'll discover your own bureau in the earth, now that the possibility has been introduced.

Example 2:

In Billy Collins' poem "Japan," the speaker describes his experience of repeatedly speaking a favorite haiku out loud as follows:

It feels like eating
the same small, perfect grape
again and again.

Can't you just feel that haiku in your mouth? Have you ever heard a haiku likened to a small, perfect grape before? I certainly haven't. By using a simile to bring together two unlike things, Collins shows us something unexpected about haiku.

Example 3:

. . . I have watched
the nation of the young, like jungle birds
that scream as they pass . . .

(from "Waiting in Line" by William Stafford)

What do you think this comparison to jungle birds reveals about how the speaker feels or thinks about the young people he is observing?

METAPHORS
Example 1:

These words
they are stones in the water

(from "These Poems" by June Jordan)

What kind of words do you think might be described as stones in the water? What words sink? What words help make a crossing?

Example 2:

It should have been the family that lasted.
Should have been my sister and my peasant mother.
But it was not. They were the affection,
not the journey. . . .

(from "The Spirit and the Soul" by Jack Gilbert)

"They were the affection, not the journey": an entirely new way of perceiving the loss of family before their time.

Example 3:

> And the cups of your breasts! And your eyes full of absence!
> And the roses of your mound! And your voice slow and sad!

(from "Body of a Woman" by Pablo Neruda, translated by Robert Bly)

Do you think these lines would be improved or weakened if Neruda had instead written:

> And your breasts like cups! And your eyes empty as absence
> And your mound like roses! And your voice slow and sad!

Why do you imagine he made the choices he made?

CHOOSING YOUR FIGURATIVE IMAGES

The poet Jack Gilbert says a simile is one of the weakest things you can do. Ted Kooser, on the other hand, defends their virtues. As with all of the craft possibilities in poetry, it will be up to you to explore where, when, and how metaphors and similes best express what you want to say in a poem.

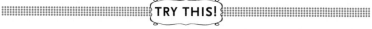

TRY THIS!

- Choose a poem, either yours or someone else's, that is sprinkled with at least a few metaphors and similes. Rewrite the poem, swapping metaphors for similes and vice versa. For example, "Her silenced smile was like a dead star" might change to "Her silenced smile was a dead star." Or, "My heart is a kite" could become "My heart lifted like a kite."

  - Notice how these changes impact the tone or meaning of the poem, if at all.

WRITING THE LIFE POETIC

- Notice how these changes impact the tone or meaning of the poem, if at all.

  - In each instance where you made a swap, decide which choice you think was better for the poem: the original or your revision.

- Keep a metaphor and simile log where you practice seeing and experiencing your world in figurative images.

  - I recommend two columns, side-by-side, where you try out every image both ways—as simile and metaphor. This will train your eye and ear over time to discern which is a better fit.

  - For a week, strive to make at least ten entries in each column of the log per day.

  - Write a poem using three to five of your favorite metaphors from this log. Then rewrite the poem swapping out the metaphors with the matching similes listed on your log. Write a final version in which you use the mix of metaphors and similes that feel right for this poem.

FOLLOW THE GOLDEN THREAD

In Haydn Reiss's documentary *William Stafford and Robert Bly: A Literary Friendship*, the two poets walk through a wintry landscape discussing poetry. Among the many topics they contemplate is the process of "following the golden thread," inspired by these lines of a William Blake poem:

> I give you the end of a golden string;
> Only wind it into a ball,
> It will lead you in at Heaven's gate,
> Built in Jerusalem's wall.

As the poets speculate that the golden string in this poem represents the idea or inspiration that leads one to the realm of poetry, Bly asks Stafford, "Do you believe that every golden thread will lead us through Jerusalem's wall, or do you love particular threads?"

Stafford replies, "No, every thread."

Stafford's response here reflects the poetic standard he taught and lived by: Any thought or idea, not just the ones we decide are good, has the potential to lead us to a poem. A champion of the humble moments that unfurl to become poems, Stafford warns not to pull the threads too hard, or the poem will be lost.

Some time after his conversation with Robert Bly, William Stafford wrote this poem:

THE WAY IT IS | BY WILLIAM STAFFORD

There's a thread that you follow. It goes among
things that change. But it doesn't change.
People wonder about what you are pursuing.
You have to explain about the thread.
But it is hard for others to see.
While you hold it you can't get lost.
Tragedies happen; people get hurt
or die; and you suffer and get old.
Nothing you can do can stop time's unfolding.
You don't ever let go of the thread.

Because a poem means something different to each person who reads
it, I will refrain from sharing my interpretation and let you decide
what this poem means to you. However, I will point out that the gold-
en string Blake offered and that Stafford and Bly discussed ultimately
made an appearance in Stafford's poem. This is a good example of
the iterative nature of poetry. It's as if poetry were a single, global,
eternal conversation all poets were having—a call and response to
each other.

Blake's poem inspired Stafford's poem through which we inherit
this imperative: *You don't ever let go of the thread.* What does this mean
to you? Let's experiment with the golden threads of our own lives
and poetry.

TRY THIS!

- Continue the call-and-response that Blake started and Stafford and Bly continued by writing a poem that incorpo-
  rates a phrase, line, or idea from either Blake's or Stafford's
  poem above.

- Take a walk with a writer friend and discuss what "the gold-
  en thread" means to each of you. At the end of the walk,
  each of you should write a poem about what you discovered.
  Share and compare your poems when you're ready.

- If you had to name one or two or three golden threads that you have always followed, what would they be?

- What golden threads has life presented you with today that you might follow into a poem? As Nuar Alsadir describes on page 71, listen to the language your mind serves up, and let it lead you to unexpected new places.

- Choose a poem written by someone else that raises an issue or introduces a possibility that intrigues you. Pick up the golden thread where that poet left off and experiment with how it might lead you into a poem of your own.

- What poet, living or dead, would you most want to walk with in the woods on a snowy day? What would you want to discuss with them? Where might the golden thread of an imaginary dialogue with this poet lead you?

"Once, while waiting tables, my mind simply said, 'Like this are the days, like this the nights, but the mornings they are different, early afternoons.' I followed it, sat at a table during my break and wrote out this poem on my order pad:

ABSINTHE | BY NUAR ALSADIR

Like this are the days
and like this the nights;

but the mornings they are different,
early afternoons.

I'm counting the ways you comfort me
like a soldier counts his legs.

In these altitudes
I forget to breathe.

I am the broken plate
over and over.

You come to me straight,
double into aside.

I'll never be here,
my throat full of night.

You sit across from me,
going blind.

The irony was that when I wrote the poem I was in what I thought was a happy relationship. I was surprised by the content, but nonetheless followed it to the end. Soon after, I realized—or allowed myself to acknowledge—the degree to which I was unhappy. The poem knew before I did. Be surprised by how much you know by listening to yourself instead of making yourself speak."

—Nuar Alsadir

℘ 21 ℘
FINDERS KEEPERS: FOUND POEMS

One day, as I was about to send a pesky spam e-mail to its untimely death, I noticed that the nonsense language was pretty interesting. I added a few line breaks, whittled out some words that didn't feel right, and presto: an instant poem. This launched a new hobby of collecting e-spam and crafting my favorite parts into poems. By using source material that I didn't write, I felt liberated from my typical thinking and writing patterns that can become dull and predictable. These poems didn't sound or feel like me. What a relief! I posted a few of the spam poems on my blog, and a few friends wrote to congratulate me on my new voice. Here's a small snippet:

> the shelf.
> double-diamond
> formation, wingtips
> almost overlapping.
> They came across
> died, mostly
> the old people,
> and not
> too many of them.
> I, for one, think
> "space."

What gems of interesting language might be hiding in your e-mail junk folder or paper recycling bin?

I also like to collect mistakes. My friend Austin brought a jacket home from Japan that says "angel potato." This linguistic faux-pas sums up for me the happy accidents of poetry; some phrase is fumbled completely, and an entirely unexpected new possibility is born. Angel potato. I see a kindergarten project, where toothpicks sunk deep in weeping, white flesh support withered, tissue-paper wings. I have always been a devotee of the potato—that otherworldly root vegetable. So unassuming and receptive to interpretation. What might happen next? Ecstatic orange? Its navel puckered into a contemplative heaven. Or: Shatter lamb. A history of cruelty and farmland. I want to know how far words can go.

I've also crafted poems out of letters badly translated from other languages, typos I've found in marketing materials, goofy slogans from the backs of cereal boxes and café chalkboards. And misunderstandings or misreadings of my own that led to accidental, often humorous, word play.

Poems that use language borrowed from someone else's writing are called "found poems." Found poems can literally use words from anything and anywhere, such as the spam e-mail. The poet then crafts new or reinvented meaning using this excerpted language. From the compost of accidents and errors rise the great blossoms of originality and surprise!

The following is a found poem composed primarily of Jane Hirshfield's genius. Because it contains so much of the poet's original language, I would never seek publication for this poem in a literary journal. I offer it here only as an example of the thrill of imitation, and what you can learn by mixing and matching the phrases and fragments of language that attract you.

OR EQUALLY, THE CITY IS BURNING
(What I learned from Jane Hirshfield)

The opposite of time is Auschwitz.
5 people, 6 griefs, the clapper

of a bell once kissed by brides
wanting children. Because I could,

I spoke: Ecstasy, Czechoslovakia, 1933.
The pebble is recalcitrant until

you take it in. Eventually
those boys will leave home.

You expect me to be
you and know you

though the knife can not divide
itself. Evolutionary pacifism:

The science of elephants.
The elephants of science.

Those who act will suffer,
suffer into truth: the truth

of the protagonist. Those
who can not act will

suffer more. The taste
of your own tongue

in your mouth as you
make yourself obsolete.

Dismantling the obvious into
its component possibilities

she stands
in a closet soon

to be empty calling
it pleasure.

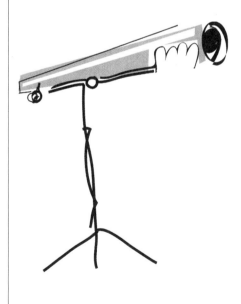

- Start saving mistakes—yours and others': funny things that someone said or wrote wrong, printed material that has a goof, even the humiliating blunders that cost someone a job, a friend, or an opportunity. There's often a lot of energy that gets pent up when we repress personal mistakes, and these can lead to rich poetic discoveries.

- Change your regard for garbage. The next time you and spam are about to part ways, dig out the gems before sending it to its virtual demise.

- Collect any English-as-a-second-language personal letters and documents from your community. Look to them to help you un-learn standard phrasings and find new ways to reinvent your relationship with language.

- Attend a poetry reading and listen as if your own poetry depended on it (because it does!). Write down any phrases or language that grab you. Later, you can use these to ignite your imagination as you craft your own poems.

ꙮ 22 ꙮ
FEARS AND FAILURES

". . . I've noticed that the primary difference
between successful people and unsuccessful
people is that the successful people fail more."

—Martha Beck

I believe that fear is the number one reason that people who are tempted to attempt poetry resist it. Somehow, by the time we've left elementary school, many of us have been socialized to believe that we are not smart enough, deep enough, interesting enough, or imaginative enough to write poetry. This wet blanket snuffs out our creative embers, reinforcing our distrust in our ability to make fire.

Ambrose Redmoon says that courage is not the absence of fear, but rather the judgment that something else is more important than fear. I recommend that you choose to make the writing of poetry more important than the fear that you may not have what it takes. The worst that can happen is you write a few poems and then move on to sudoko, right?

Every beginning, intermediate, and advanced poet bumbles around, flails and even fails. Just as you must crawl before you walk, and then you must bonk your head on multiple inanimate objects as you make the transition toward bipedal grace, you are going to have triumphs and tumbles as you endeavor to write poems. For more than twenty years, I have been writing poems and thinking of each one as practice. Writing is a lifelong craft, and not a moment of it is wasted. Every poem you write benefits from the poems that came before it.

- (This is a writing exercise from Shanna Germain.) Write a horrible poem. Just as horrible as you can. Filled with all the mistakes you're afraid of making, all the clichés that you hate, all the things your teachers have told you never to put into poems. Once you have done this, once you have written the horrible thing you're always afraid you're going to write and you've looked it in the face, you can move on. Often, even in writing that horrible poem, there's a glimpse of the true good thing that makes you want to be a poet. There's a nice bit of voice, or a lovely off rhyme, or an image that comes through.

- Sift through your pile of reject poems. That's right: the ones that most humiliate you. Fetch them from your garbage can and un-crumple them, then sit down with a red pen and circle a word, phrase, image, line break, sound—*something*—that you admire in each poem. Create a new document where you save all of these little fragments of success. Refer back to them the next time you're feeling discouraged to remind yourself of the potential in every compost heap. You may even want to use one as a starting point for a new poem. (See chapter seventy for more ideas about repurposing the slush pile.)

Failing and Flying | by Jack Gilbert

Everyone forgets that Icarus also flew.
It's the same when love comes to an end,
or the marriage fails and people say
they knew it was a mistake, that everybody
said it would never work. That she was
old enough to know better. But anything
worth doing is worth doing badly.
Like being there by that summer ocean
on the other side of the island while
love was fading out of her, the stars
burning so extravagantly those nights that
anyone could tell you they would never last.
Every morning she was asleep in my bed
like a visitation, the gentleness in her
like antelope standing in the dawn mist.
Each afternoon I watched her coming back
through the hot stony field after swimming,
the sea light behind her and the huge sky
on the other side of that. Listened to her
while we ate lunch. How can they say
the marriage failed? Like the people who
came back from Provence (when it was Provence)
and said it was pretty but the food was greasy.
I believe Icarus was not failing as he fell,
but just coming to the end of his triumph.

THE FACES OF THE STRANGER

"I'm always living the masked me. I use poetry
to get out of the way—and let my essence come
through. I was surprised to read recently that
the word larva is derived from the word mask.
One of these says I will emerge as a butterfly."

—Sue Einowski

Each day demands of us a jumble of situation-specific identities, each with its own uniform, tone of voice, and persona. Mostly without even thinking about it, we modulate who we are to reflect the relationship we are in. Our spouse, mother, child, boss, and best friend each know a slightly different version of us, defined by the context of that relationship. For example, you probably don't talk or dress at work as you do at home. And the story about getting pulled over for running a stop sign while questionably tipsy would likely be told differently to your reckless teenage son, your judgmental father, and your commiserating girlfriend. Then there are those parts of you that don't seem fit for public viewing by anyone, even the people to whom you are closest.

This cultural schizophrenia that we all suffer is rich with possibilities for your writing life. We all have a stranger (in fact, a chorus of strangers) inside us. Poetry gives you a vehicle for getting acquainted with your inner strangers, unveiling what is hidden, experimenting with your masks, and fashioning the fractioned subsets of who you believe yourself to be into your own interpreted, multifaceted wholes.

In effect, poetry can be a kind of masquerade ball, through which you play out and make sense of affairs, deaths, emotional wounds, incapacitating fears, and secrets. Don't forget the ecstatic masks;

through poetry, you can vicariously breathe in trees, travel through time, discover new truths, and love as if there were no tomorrow.

I chose poetry for its masks and unmaskings. The poem was the arrow I followed into the heart of the human condition—to be touched by someone whose pain or truth was entirely different from mine . . . or quite similar. I tried on every mask I was given, and poetry became my portal into the world and into myself. How can it unveil you?

TRACKS | BY MARGE PIERCY

The small birds leave cuneiform
messages on the snow: I have
been here, I am hungry, I
must eat. Where I dropped
seeds they scrape down
to pine needles and frozen sand.

Sometimes when snow flickers
past the windows, muffles trees
and bushes, buries the path,
the jays come knocking with their beaks
on my bedroom window:
to them I am made of seeds.

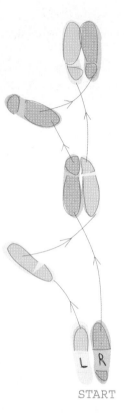

To the cats I am mother and lover,
lap and toy, cook and cleaner.
To the coyotes I am chaser and shouter.
To the crows, watcher, protector.
To the possums, the foxes, the skunks,
a shadow passing, a moment's wind.

I was bad watchful mommy to one man.
To another I was forgiving sister
whose hand poured out honey and aloe;
to that woman I was a gale whose lashing
waves threatened her foundation; to this
one, an oak to her flowering vine.

I have worn the faces, the masks
of hieroglyphs, gods and demons,
bat-faced ghosts, sibyls and thieves,
lover, loser, red rose and ragweed,
these are the tracks I have left
on the white crust of time.

Define your inner chorus. Identify the cast of masked characters comprising you, and then put them to work in your poems.

- Name six masks you wear; strive for a mix of the obvious and the previously undisclosed. Don't be afraid to be unflattering; the bare bulb of truth is often the most interesting.

- Give each mask a celebrity name. Bono, Cher, Beyoncé, and Madonna have become cultural icons recognizable by their one-word names. If you were to choose your own celebrity name for each mask—a word or phrase that communicates to the world what is most fabulous or memorable about this particular aspect of you—what would it be?

- How would you categorize each mask by texture? Which ones are satin, steel, silk, leather, corduroy, flannel, lace, barbed wire?

- Write a poem from the point of view of one masked character. (Let's say, "Smiling Soccer Mom.") Use your chosen texture in the poem.

- Now reinvent the same poem from the point of view of one of your masks at the other end of the spectrum. (How about "Vixen of Vitriol"?) What does Smiling Soccer Mom say, see, and do that Vixen of Vitriol would never consider? And what ground does Vixen cover that Soccer Mom wouldn't dream of setting foot on?

❧24❧
SOUND: WRITING OUT LOUD

I wrote and read poems for about a decade in complete secrecy before ever taking a class or reading a how-to book. In that time, I regret to say, I missed out on the appreciation (or at least the conscious appreciation) of sound in poetry. I didn't read my poems out loud; I had no idea how they sounded spoken. "Writing by ear" was a possibility that had never occurred to me.

Then, by a stroke of good fortune, I ended up in a class with Robert Bly where we each stood up, read poems out loud, and tried to find where the vowels were sounding in our body. It was as if I'd suddenly flipped a switch and the world of poetry went from two-dimensional to three-dimensional. Poetry was *music*! It was meant to be read OUT LOUD! It was received in both the body and the mind! I felt good when sounds repeated! Bingo.

The bottom line is that sound in poetry matters. Repeating sounds are pleasurable for the reader, and can help create a sense of unity and music in the poem. (Though sometimes too many repeating sounds can be distracting or bring us a bit closer than we'd like to Mother Goose.) The trick is to experiment with sound until you know what feels right to you.

Let's take a look at the choices I made in the opening lines of my poem "Exfoliation":

A chorus of fat nervous birds
jitters on the rim of my table.

First, read them out loud. What do you notice about the sound? How many repeating sounds can you find? I'll point out just a few examples of ways in which the words echo each other. In the stanza below, each shape represents a different sound. This is called a *sound diagram.*

A chorus of fat nervous birds
jitters on the rim of my table

Notice how many t's and r's and o's there are here? A mix of internal rhymes, and repeating consonant and vowel sounds helps these lines feel like they belong together.

I didn't write these lines by formula, but by feel—and sound. After I complete a draft, I go back through and clean up the sound, exploring ways to replace words that don't sound "of a piece" with the rest of the poem. Another poet might have chosen something more like this, with the repeating sounds in "distressed" and "edge" creating a slightly different music:

A chorus of fat distressed birds
jitters on the edge of my table

By making deliberate choices about the music of a line, you'll attune yourself to make such choices automatically and intuitively over time. It's similar to progressing from practicing scales on a new instrument to playing an improvisational solo once you've developed some proficiency. The more you practice the more fluent you become.

TRY THIS!

- How would you complete these lines to create your own great sounding lines?

    A _____ of fat _____ birds
    _____ on the _____ of my table

- Read the poem on the next page out loud, slowly. As you read it, pay attention to where the vowel sounds resonate in your body. Which echo in your chest, throat, nose, belly, head? Which feel like the most natural and pleasing sounds to you?

Alchemy | by Sage Cohen

Consequence and its heavy metals strive toward
    transformation
while imprecisely, a silent pine resonates with lake.

Among the assurances of proximity and place, she floats out,
weightless, over the lake's flat gaze. Heavy arms repeated
    and relieved.

Birds shape themselves to wind. The trees shift,
shimmering as snow sifts its silences.

Shadows send their slender semiselves out like wishes
that have not yet learned to lift. I sit doubled beside the pine.

A woman pleads with me from within the lake: *Leave*—
Listening to her is like eating a peach right down to the pit.

Everything green folds to gold and starts again.
Leaden is the death that does not find its way forward.

Harmony must first have been an opposition that stumbled
into agreement slightly above the departure.

- Take out a pen, and make a sound diagram of "Alchemy" by circling each repeating sound in a different color. (I chose a shorter poem so you can easily copy it into your notebook and do the diagram there if you're not comfortable writing directly in this book.)

- Do a sound diagram of one of your own poems. Notice which of the sounds you naturally repeated. Swap out three words with synonyms that are a better fit for the sound of the poem.

- Robert Bly once insisted that if there aren't at least three repeating sounds in every line of a poem, it's not a poem. Write a poem that would make Bly proud.

25

LEARN A FOREIGN LANGUAGE (OR CREATE YOUR OWN)

Poetry demands, invites, cajoles, and implores us to experience language in new ways. A great way to stretch the waistband of your imagination and make room for a more inventive relationship with language is to grow your vocabulary in new directions and find surprising, new ways of experiencing the words you already know. In poetry, even inventing your own language is an option.

GROW YOUR VOCABULARY

At a reading I attended many years ago, Galway Kinnell was asked by an audience member, "If you had just one piece of advice for beginning poets, what would it be?" Galway replied simply, "Learn the names of things." As writers, becoming intimate with the physical world involves taking it in with our senses and then processing it through language.

Every industry, sport, and hobby has its own culture and vocabulary. Tackle some new activity and you'll discover a world of words that you may never have encountered before. At a salmon hatchery, you're likely to hear: anadromous, trolling, milt, and riffle. On a writing retreat in the heart of a community founded on the logging trade, I discovered lumberjack lingo of the Pacific Northwest: gyppo, kerf, jillpoke, and peavey. Fresh to my ear and inviting on the page, the language of the timber industry led me into an exploration of its history through poetry.

Ballerinas, horseback riders, stamp collectors, quilters, bowlers, and downhill skiers each have their own unique vocabularies for defining their special expertise. Expand your knowledge base by reading a book or taking a class, joining an online chat group, or just doing something new. Then see where the language leads you.

INVENT YOUR OWN LANGUAGE

Urban legend claims that the Eskimo have hundreds of words for "snow." What topic or phenomenon do you know a whole lot about? Love? The theory of relativity? Grasshoppers? Ultimate Frisbee?

Invent ten new words that express the various facets of your topic. For example, maybe there's a word for the summer trill of grasshopper song and another word describing the fragile optimism of a grasshopper's leap. Write a poem using at least three words from your new vocabulary.

GET LOST (AND FOUND) IN TRANSLATION

Find a poem in a language you don't know. "Translate" each word based on an English word it sounds like or reminds you of. The goal is to let sound trigger words without worrying about literal translation or even making sense.

For example:

> **Pablo Neruda, from "Aquí"**
>
> Me vine aquí a contar las campanas
>
> **Sage Cohen "sound translation"**
>
> My vine aqua a contrary last camp annals

I never would have composed anything like this line if left to my own devices. That's the point—to get outside your linguistic bag of tricks, and see what aqua vines await you.

MAKE A LINGUISTIC PEANUT BUTTER CUP

Remember those old Reese's Peanut Butter Cup commercials where they dramatize the discovery of the candy? A man holding a bar of chocolate stumbles into a man holding a jar of peanut butter. Subsequent to their irritation at this unexpected merger, both men delight in the taste revelation of chocolate plus peanut butter, exclaiming: "Two great tastes that taste great together!"

Such happy accidents are also possible with language. The word "brunch," for example, is the hinge where "breakfast" swivels into "lunch." The trendy word "guesstimate" interlaces "guess" and "estimate." "Smog" was born of "smoke" and "fog." I have a new favorite:

In the movie *What Would Jesus Buy?*, a protest against American consumerism, Reverend Billy of the Church of Stop Shopping coins the word "Shopocalypse," conflating "shop" and "apocalypse."

These invented words that break open and weave together two words or ideas into a new, integrated composition are called portmanteau words, after a portmanteau suitcase that opens up into two hinged compartments. If you were going to create your own linguistic peanut butter cup, what two great tastes would you combine into a single word? What might writing a poem composed primarily of portmanteau words teach you about sound, meaning, and the endless potential of language?

REWRITE THE DICTIONARY

Lohren Green's poetry collection, *Poetical Dictionary*, features poems that breathe new life into standard dictionary definitions. Following is one of my favorites:

> **oyster-** intangibly mouth, then
> cinch a sense: "oi'st ər"
> *n.* [From Greek *óstreon*,
> distinguishing it
> by its Greek *óstrakon*, hard
> shell, *ostéon* bone]
> I. gills sip oceans
> (or seas)
> into the delicate
> bulges of a
> liquor-glossed life
> pulled plush
> by the stick
> of brine salts
> and slumped
> inside a two-bone
> cloister.

What dictionary definitions might you improve upon through a poetic reinterpretation? Choose three words from a dictionary: one you admire, one you've never heard before, and one that has never appealed to you. Write a poem about each. See where this leads you.

～26～
SMALL STONES

*". . . I decided to look for a small stone every day
for a year . . . They are nothing special and
something special all at once. As time went
on, I got better at remembering to notice the
world around me. Not just to notice it but to
scrutinize it, engage with it, love it. My eyes,
ears, nose, mouth and hands opened up."*

—Fiona Robyn

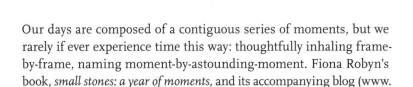

Our days are composed of a contiguous series of moments, but we rarely if ever experience time this way: thoughtfully inhaling frame-by-frame, naming moment-by-astounding-moment. Fiona Robyn's book, *small stones: a year of moments*, and its accompanying blog (www. asmallstone.com), reminded me of the great wealth of poetic source material every ordinary day presents us with.

In both Robyn's book and blog, she offers readers "small stones." These brief sentences or paragraphs offer palpable moments of carefully observed grace. (Please see page 92 for examples.) In each, Robyn gives us something deeply perceived and fully felt. It's as if we are offered again and again a cup of sustenance from the source that is language itself.

What if we were to follow Robyn's example and choose a "small stone" as a place marker for each day—a little glimpse into the wonder of life through the portal of a single thing or scene studied carefully? From the glittering to the bruised, the mundane to the magnificent, we might find our days and our world far more intimate and engaging places to inhabit.

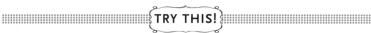

- Designate a "small stones" day in which you invite wonder into your dialogue with your experience. Consider each moment as a single jewel strung on a necklace, or a stone strewn on a path. Three times throughout the day, pay attention to a single, ordinary thing, and write it down.

  - For one "stone," consider something in nature.

  - For another, observe yourself in relationship with someone or something.

  - And finally, seek out something that you might not otherwise notice because your mind filters it out as litter, inconvenience, or a waste of time.

- Keep a "small stones" journal in which you challenge yourself to capture one brief, poetic moment or image per day.

- Invite your friends into your small stones practice:

  - Gather with a group of ten or more people and do something to invigorate your imaginations: walk outside, study a few pieces of art, conjure meaningful memories through free writing, or do whatever feels most stimulating to the group.

  - On index cards, invite each person to write five poetic fragments or small stones (one per card).

  - Put all of the small stones in a single pile and invite each person to choose three (not their own) that particularly speak to her.

  - Sit down in a circle either facing each other or facing away from each other. (You might want to try this both ways, as each yields interesting and varied results.) Have a designated person read a small stone out loud.

- Invite anyone who has chosen a piece of writing that resonates with the first stone to then read her stone out loud. Then invite the rest of the group to do the same, following the resonance stone by stone until each one has been spoken.

- Take ten minutes to each write something in response to your experience of choosing, reading, and then listening to the relationship among the small stones of others.

Fiona Robyn's Small Stones

January
The sun sags in the sky. Half a lemon sits face down in a puddle, scenting the water with citrus. Everything tightens against the cold.

April
A digger tips its scoop: the sand slides out as if from a cupped palm

July
Lie on your back on the grass, become quiet. One by one, they step forward. The chopped circle of the moon. Honeysuckle scent edging the breeze. Swallows weaving counterpoint, and above them an aeroplane in poor imitation. And next door's roses, punching holes into the evening, as red as the reddest lipstick.

September
Sky bites: not pieces of sky, cool-blue and smooth in your palm, but oddments of pretzel nuggets covered in sesame, raisins, moss-green pumpkin seeds, sealed in plastic and handed out at thirty-thousand feet.

∽ 27 ∽
IMITATION IS THE HIGHEST
FORM OF DISCOVERY

Intimidation is one of the fastest ways to poison the seeds of poetic possibility. We all know the drill: "I'll never be as good as [fill in the blank of whatever famous poet you most admire here], so why bother?"

Let's face it—you're right. You're not going to ever write like anyone but you. But that's the beauty of it. One Whitman, one Dickinson, one Frost is enough. They each did their part. Now it's your turn to do yours. Let's leave our heroes on our bookshelves, where they belong. But first, let's raid their wardrobe, try on their shoes and bow ties and raincoats, and see what fits. By imitating shamelessly whatever you like best about others' work, you may discover new ways of using sound, language, imagery, and form that you hadn't considered previously.

Most of us are taught that imitation is the death of originality. In my experience, the opposite is true. Paradoxically, when I was teaching a university undergraduate creative writing class, the imitation exercises yielded the most interesting, inspiring, and original results of the entire semester. Somehow, aligning themselves with work they admired helped these young poets break through to their own authentic, powerful voices—with maybe a few echoes of the poems they were imitating. In the same way that wearing an Incredible Hulk costume on Halloween might acquaint you with your inner, gigantic green muscle machine, trying on other poets' approaches and sensibilities can help you explore different dimensions of who you are and what you have to say.

In Paulann Petersen's Second Sight workshop, she described her first realization that a poem she was reading was titled with a phrase excerpted from a line in the poem. Before this discovery, Paulann said it hadn't occurred to her that a poet had such a simple, easy option. I remember my surprise the first time I read numbered stanzas; and what a thrill it was to learn from E.E. Cummings that the rules of punctuation do not necessarily apply in poetry. In fact, each poem you read teaches you something new about what is possible in poetry. That's why imitation is invaluable; it can open the escape hatch from rules you weren't even aware you were abiding by. As you strive to repeat something you admire, you unlock greater possibilities for the poetry you write. The deeper you travel into someone else's writing, the more likely you are to discover what is most alive and engaging in your own.

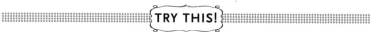

TRY THIS!

- Sit down with a favorite poem and read it out loud a few times.

- Write down three things you admire about it, such as the title, theme, shape of lines and stanzas, sound, imagery, language choices, capitalization, etc. Be as detailed as possible about *why* you admire the choices the poet made and how you feel these benefit the poem.

- Did you discover anything about "what's allowed" in poetry that you hadn't realized before?

- Write a poem that employs the three techniques you admired. It doesn't have to be a similar topic or theme to the poem you are imitating—unless you want it to be.

- Notice how your poem is like and unlike the original poem that inspired it.

28

THE STARVING ARTIST HAS LEFT THE BUILDING: ON POETRY AND PROSPERITY

*"It is a sad fact about our culture that a poet
can earn much more money writing or talking
about his art than he can by practicing it."*

—W.H. Auden

When I majored in comparative literature as an undergraduate, my friend Jayne's father, an accountant, asked me what kind of job I intended to land with such an ambiguous degree. "It will teach me how to think, and I'll be good at any number of jobs if I'm a capable thinker," I countered. His sons and daughter were getting practical degrees: accounting, journalism, medicine. Each knew what he or she would do with their education. Jayne's father shrugged his shoulders and wished me luck.

Five years later when I was a year into a master's degree in creative writing, Jayne's father asked me why in the world I would get such a useless degree and how I intended to make a living when I graduated. The smart aleck in me responded, "I'm going to marry your son Abe, and he's going to support me." Jayne's father never inquired about my career path again.

I think this conversation reflects a typical cultural fear: If you pursue the arts, you will starve. You will become anachronistic and ill-suited for the workplace. No one will hire you. End of story. This is why many a parent has discouraged many a poet over the years from embracing such impractical passions. (I was blessed with parents who were poets and writers themselves and celebrated my love of the written word.)

I never bought into the starving artist archetype. For me, starving is no fun. Being penniless is a grind. Just as you can't plant potatoes on a bridge, it's hard to build a creative practice on a life that has no foundation on solid ground. A roof over my head and the certainty of being able to pay my monthly expenses have always been the foundation of my creativity.

When writing poetry, there's a very simple way to sidestep the starving artist archetype: Don't expect to make a living writing poetry. Jayne's father was right: Most poets don't make a living writing poetry. But this doesn't exclude poets from prosperity. While it's easy to lump money and prosperity together, I propose that you don't. Instead, I'd like you to consider how you define prosperity. For me, a leisurely afternoon in a coffee shop with a pile of poetry books, a notebook and a pen, and a regular refill of tea is prosperity. A good conversation with a friend is prosperity. My dog licking my face is prosperity.

This is not to say that we who write poetry are somehow above earning a good income. I'm just pointing out that income is one thing, and prosperity is frequently something else. Wallace Stevens, one of the most wildly imaginative poets on record, was an insurance adjustor by day. William Carlos Williams was a pediatrician. Mari L'Esperance is a therapist. The great blessing of poetry is that a "day job" can't take poetry away from you. If you love poetry, you find a time to write it, no matter what else you're doing, no matter how much time or energy or mental exhaustion that other commitment wrings out of you.

I have a marketing communications writing business that supports my creative writing craft. I find that when I'm really cranking with my business writing, often my creative writing is flying high, right alongside it. Many poets teach. Some who are renowned are paid well to read and speak publicly. Others feel that they must do work for money that does not engage their creative mind at all. David Sedaris, for example, launched his writing empire telling the stories of the hilarious odd jobs he did to support his career as a writer. It's all grist for the mill, as they say!

You simply need to know what prosperity means to you and then create a balance of what you do for money and what you do for poetry. This will help you stay creatively awake, engaged, and enthralled with all dimensions of your working and creative life.

29

MAKING MUSIC: RHYME, RHYTHM, AND REPETITION

"I've been asked a lot recently about the difference
between writing poems and writing song lyrics
and have disappointed a few people, including
myself, by reminding them that there may not
be all that much in the way of difference . . ."

—Paul Muldoon

Songs can take hold of us and refuse to let go. I have been taken hostage for days, years, decades by some of my favorites. I'll bet you have, too. What do songs do that speaks so directly to us and moves us so deeply?

In songs, rhyme, rhythm, and repetition typically work together to deliver messages in a way that we respond to physically and emotionally—so much so that hearing a song can spin us back to the time and place of our first hearing it—resurfacing smells, feelings, even people who we might not otherwise have remembered. It seems, then, that the songs we love somehow plug into our nervous systems, entangling themselves in our memories. Because songs are poems set to music, we have the same opportunities to tickle people down to their foundations with the rhymes, rhythms, and repetitions we choose in our poems.

RHYME
In chapter twenty-four we talked about the pleasures of repeating sounds, and their capacity to create a kind of cohesion in a poem.

This is the delight of rhyme; it's easier to retain a phrase if it is strung together with sounds that echo each other, probably because it feels good to say and hear it.

RHYTHM

Songs rely heavily on instruments to communicate rhythm; poems use words and lines and white space. But the trajectory is similar. The way you break a line, space a stanza, and choose your words for their syllabic pluck is akin to the drum keeping a beat for a song. Chapters thirty-three and thirty-four discuss in detail how lines and stanzas can establish the momentum of a poem.

REPETITION

Most songs have a chorus—a catchy few phrases that get repeated intermittently throughout. When done successfully, a chorus creates a kind of comforting return to the familiar, while expanding in meaning each time as the song progresses. Repetition can work the same way in free-verse poems, but with no standard formula to follow. The real craft of repetition comes in offering something fresh with each appearance, using a recurring idea or image to peel back layer after layer, rather than circling the reader back to the same idea, of which he will tire easily. Consider how beautifully Jane Kenyon Kenyon's poem and Drew Pearce's song lyrics make an impact through repetition:

LET EVENING COME | BY JANE KENYON

Let the light of late afternoon
shine through chinks in the barn, moving
up the bales as the sun moves down.

Let the cricket take up chafing
as a woman takes up her needles
and her yarn. Let evening come.

Let dew collect on the hoe abandoned
in long grass. Let the stars appear
and the moon disclose her silver horn.

Let the fox go back to its sandy den.
Let the wind die down. Let the shed
go black inside. Let evening come.

To the bottle in the ditch, to the scoop
in the oats, to air in the lung
let evening come.

Let it come, as it will, and don't
be afraid. God does not leave us
comfortless, so let evening come.

DARRINGTON | BY DREW PEARCE

On the road between the riverbed and the waterlogged white bark,
the rusted-out yellow bus has been permanently parked
in the cold, wet shadow of a February Darrington day.
Inside, you're sleeping on the floor, riding out the gray,
dreaming what it was that drove you out this way

You try to see a reason hidden underneath such a random spark
A vein of lightning where the clouds collide leaves you counting
  in the dark

You come home, close the curtains on a rainy afternoon
Open them back up to see the waning cheshire moon
You keep yourself surrounded with what was left behind
Dakota arrowheads, maple petrified, two feet underground,
easier than you would be to find

You try to see a reason hidden underneath such a random spark
A vein of lightning where the clouds collide leaves you counting
  in the dark
A vein of lightning where the clouds collide stops another brother's heart

But you could still wake up, still light enough to see,
Walk along the river bank right across the street.
You could ferry cross the sound, look up at the sky,

See something so beautiful you feel like crying
Because in spite of what you hear, in spite of what you see,
in spite of what you fear, in spite of what you need,
Good things go on happening, and it's okay

Don't bottle yourself up, don't fold yourself inside,
Don't throw yourself on the mercy of the retreating tide
You've been locked away. Don't wait to be released.
You can open it yourself. You can let yourself be free
You're still alive enough to give love and be loved.
You're still alive enough to let yourself be loved.

Notice how both writers build emotional tension. How do rhyme, rhythm and repetition work together to convey meaning?

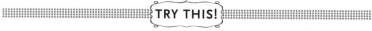

TRY THIS!

- Modeled on song lyrics, write a poem that has end rhymes, similar syllable-count lines, and possibly even a recurring chorus. Use Drew Pearce's "Darrington" as your template. Or choose a song by Ani DiFranco, Drew Pearce, Leonard Cohen, Lucinda Williams, Box Set, Paul Simon, Joni Mitchell, Bono, Austin Willacy, Bruce Springsteen, or any artist whose lyrics you've admired and connected with as your template and accomplice. Don't be shy about imitating. Notice what types of poems want to come through you in this format.

- Write a poem that repeats a word or phrase as it develops an idea or feeling. Try exploring a big concept that is hard to define, like death, freedom, or grief. Look to Kenyon's and Rich's poems as examples.

- What song lyrics stir you up every time you hear them? How do you think the song accomplishes this? Is it the subject matter, the tone, the sound? What does the poem behind the music have to teach you about your own unsung poems? Write a poem that strives to create in its reader the same reaction you have to this moving song.

✒ 30 ✒
REDEFINING "REAL WORK"

"We live in a society in which 'work' is
synonymous with tangible 'product' (and
monetary compensation certainly falls
into this category). As a poet, one spends
necessary time (when one can get it!)
mulling, daydreaming, and internally
composting. What looks like idleness is,
in fact, 'work' and is absolutely necessary
to the 'product.' To most in the greater
culture, however, this is not 'work' at all;
only the 'product' (the poem, in particular
the PUBLISHED poem ...) is considered of
any real value ... I've learned over the years
that I, and no one else, have to believe in the
value of my own creative process, something
that is unique for each artist. In the end,
this is what matters."

—Mari L'Esperance

A few years ago, I was fortunate to be awarded a month-long writing retreat where lodging was provided in a beautiful, shared house in the woods. As I was preparing for my month of intensely focused writing, I learned few people appreciate that unpaid work is, nonetheless, still work. The concept of a writing residency didn't make sense to most of the folks I know. Everyone from dear friends to colleagues wished me a great vacation. At least three wanted to come visit me during my "month off," dovetailing their vacation with mine.

I understood that my intention to write eight hours a day without having to think about anything or anyone from my "real life"—and without earning a cent in the process—was an alien concept to them.

"This is not a vacation," I tried to explain. "It is a chance to do personal work that means far more than any financial reward could ever offer."

"What do you owe in exchange for your month?" they asked.

"Nothing," I said. "I owe myself the opportunity to dedicate my time and effort to my own writing for a change."

This, too, drew a blank.

For the most part, the writing I do for love exists in the very small margin around the writing I do for money. Most of the people I know don't have two parallel careers: one that pays a living and another that makes living worthwhile. They can't imagine sacrificing a month of income to do something that has no probable financial (or for that matter practical) return for either the participant or the organization funding the retreat. Shaped by societal expectations, many writers are also challenged by this concept. It's not easy to give ourselves the space we need to create when we feel pressured to do "real work." Such perceptions need amending.

While doing creative work that is not shaped or defined in any way by commerce may come with certain annoyances (such as the afore-mentioned misunderstandings), it also brings great freedoms. Because it is rare to be paid for poetry, especially early in one's journey, you do not owe anything to anyone but yourself. With no agent, publisher, or public demanding a certain kind of poem, you get to determine the terms under which you write, and the poems that you create. You may choose to write poems for a certain audience, in the hopes of com-municating something specific to that audience, or you may choose to simply please yourself. How you write your poems and for what purpose are entirely up to you.

On the flip side, poetry's exemption from commerce means that the people around you may not appreciate or value poetry—or un-derstand this "so-called work" that you are taking so seriously. You could let other people's misunderstandings and stereotypes about who poets are and what they do thwart you, but I don't recommend it. The beauty of the labor of poetry is that you get to define what comprises real work for you.

READ THE POETRY YOU LOVE

*"You can't write from a vacuum any more than
you can live in one. Reading poetry is one-half
of your participation in the great pan-historical,
global conversation, and you can't afford to be
choosy. Read everything."*

—Sadie Kohler

There's no way around it: Writing poetry flows out of reading poetry.
Just as the moon collects the sun's light and pours it back into the
night sky, you must breathe in poetry to breathe it back out. This is a
fancy way of saying: Read poems! A good reading ritual is the most
direct and most satisfying way to discover the expansive range of
what's possible in poetry.

My first serious venture into poetry as a teenager was accompanied
by Marge Piercy's *The Moon Is Always Female*. I didn't know it then,
but I was seeking guidance on how one becomes a woman and how
one navigates the dynamics of intimate relationships. It was years
before I would understand that writing myself into womanhood was
going to be my path. Following Marge Piercy's trail of breadcrumbs,
I claimed several of her poems as personal anthems, taping "To have
without holding" and "For strong women" to my bedroom mirror—
and referring to them as reference points that became as reassuring
as my own reflection.

Often, you don't know what you need from poetry until you start
reading it. Over time, I have learned that I read poetry to be moved,
informed, transformed. I like to see what is possible with language,

and to find a way outside of my own ways of thinking. I like to see myself. I like to see beyond myself.

There is no better way to learn poetry than to read it, listen to it, and experience it. Poetry instructs you beyond your own personal (and school-taught) prisons of "possible" and "not possible." Even as it gives you rules, poetry breaks the rules. This is, perhaps, why poetry is so elusive. In a culture where we like things black and white, right and wrong, poetry says YES. What if there were no right or wrong—only poetry? What if everything we could possibly dream up were acceptable? Fabulous? Enough? Poetry can be your own personal oasis of invention, where you can do no wrong.

TRY THIS!

Reading poetry you love begins with simply reading poetry until you find something that clicks. Here are a few ideas for getting started:

- Ask friends, neighbors, or colleagues who read poetry what they recommend, and why.

- Attend poetry readings in your community. If you like the featured poet's work and they have books to sell, purchase one. Or ask the poets you admire what books have been important to them and see if those books also appeal to you.

- Spend a few hours at your local bookstore or library exploring its poetry section, small press section, and literary journal section. If you feel overwhelmed by the selection, try randomly pulling a book from the shelf, open to any page, and read. Repeat until you land on poetry that pleases you.

- Ask the bookstore or library folks to steer you toward the poetry they recommend, or what's popular lately. Ask if there are any local poets' books or anthologies on the shelves. In Oregon there are at least three celebrated local anthologies: *VoiceCatcher* features the work of Portland-area women writers; *Broken Word* grew out of an open-mic night, showcasing the poems of this spoken word community; and *Deer Drink*

the Moon celebrates Oregon's rich natural resources by fea-
tureing poets whose poems honor the "spirit of place." If
there is such a publication in your community, it could be
the perfect place to dive in to your poetry pursuit.

- If at first you don't succeed, try, try again. If you don't like
  what you hear or read the first or second or third time, fear
  not. Just like you're not going to like every ice cream flavor,
  it may take you a while to find the right flavor of poetry for
  your palate.

- Each time you read a poem you admire, write down one
  thing you observe about the poem that you'd like to try in
  your own poetry. The more you know about what you like,
  the more you'll be able to enjoy seeking out, reading, and
  imitating poetry.

32

GROW YOUR OWN WRITING GROUP

*"Donald Hall and I have been sending poems
back and forth twice a week for forty years ...
My generation did a lot with letters. Galway
Kinnell and Louis Simpson and Don and I
and James Wright would often send five- and
six-page letters commenting on and arguing
with each other's poems. I'm amazed we had
the time for that ... The gist of it is that no one
writes alone: One needs a community."*

—Robert Bly

Throughout the history of poetry, long before there were academic creative writing programs, poets have shared their poems with other poets and have given each other feedback. There are many ways to do this. As Robert Bly describes above, you could write a six-page commentary on a friend's poem and drop it in the mail. Or, you could gather in a small, informal group at regular intervals to read and respond to each other's work. Writing groups (also commonly called workshops) can keep you engaged in an ongoing writing and reading practice.

The primary advantage of participating in a writing group is accountability. Most of us write more when there's a deadline and write better if we know people we respect will be reading our poems. Writing groups can give you structure and a built-in audience to keep you striving for your best work. They can also give you feedback to help you learn when you're connecting with readers in the way you would like.

Another important benefit of being in a writing group is learning how to think and talk critically about poems. By spending time with a friend's poem and working to articulate what is succeeding, what needs improvement and why, you will start to develop a poetic language through which you will become familiar with your own aesthetic. Studying other people's poems and then applying what you've learned to your own work will help you hone your poetic sensibilities.

TIPS FOR A POSITIVE WRITING GROUP EXPERIENCE

Find a dedicated group of poets whose writing you admire.
Invite three to five friends who enjoy writing poetry to commit to a regular poetry group. Decide as a group how frequently you will meet. Once a month on a weekend for two or three hours is typical.

Do a thorough critique in advance of each meeting.

- A week before the meeting date, each group member e-mails the poems for discussion that month. This gives everyone time to read each other's work and come to the group prepared.

- Spend fifteen to twenty minutes with each poem you receive and write down everything you notice and admire about the poem's use of language, image, sound, voice, point of view, title, rhythm, line, etc. Chapter thirty-nine offers a list of craft issues to consider when revising a poem. If you're not sure how to begin critiquing, try running each poem you review through this filter.

- Remember that saying you like something in a poem is far less effective than actually describing what you find successful and why. Bring your notes with you to the meeting.

Speak, listen to, and learn from each other with care.
At the meeting, each member's poem is discussed for the same amount of time. If there are four members meeting for two hours, for example, the group should spend a half hour considering each poem. Everyone's turn will go something like this:

- The poet reads her piece out loud as the rest of the group reads along. Then a second person reads that same poem, so the poet can hear the poem in another voice.

- Before the conversation begins, the poet may mention any challenges or issues she would like to hear the group address.

- Group members give specific, detailed feedback about the poem, focusing on the positive as much as possible. Knowing what's working in a poem can help a poet build on strengths and stay engaged in the delight of writing poetry. Of course, knowing where readers get stuck or confused is also valuable.

- The "I" of any poem is referred to as "the speaker" and no one assumes that the poem is literally about an experience that happened to the poet (see chapter fourteen).

- This is very important: The poet does not speak throughout the conversation. She does not defend or explain her choices or argue with the opinions of others. Nor does she answer questions about what she intended. She simply listens to and observes what her friends found successful and where they struggled. For example, if she thought a metaphor was clear and each person in the group believes it means something different, she learns where revising may be necessary.

- At the end of the discussion of her piece, the writer collects the copies of her poem that include other members' notes. The group moves on to the next poet's work.

Over time, members of your writing group will get to know each other's writing styles and sensibilities. The more familiar you and your peers are with teach other's writing, the more useful you'll be in providing meaningful, constructive feedback that furthers your craft.

33

WORK THE WHITE SPACE:
SHAPING POEMS WITH LINE

Lines act as the engine that moves the reader through a poem. How you choose to hinge one line to the next, where you break the line, and the amount of white space you create through line lengths instruct the reader about how fast and bumpy—or smooth and leisurely—the ride of your poem will be.

The choices you make about lines are so individual that if the ten most recent poets laureate were each given the same paragraph and asked to break it into lines and stanzas, each would do so differently based on his or her unique sense of rhythm, music, and meaning. While there are no rules about how and where you should break lines, there are a few things you might want to consider.

Think of the line break (the place where the line ends) as a comma—the place where the reader lingers an extra beat. A line break can coincide with the completion of an idea, or it can leave the reader hanging mid-idea, intrigued and wanting more. Each creates a different kind of momentum. When breaking a line, decide what word you want the reader's eye to linger on a little longer. Because strong images or language can engage the reader enough to follow to the next line, you might want to end a line with a descriptive word like "atrophy" rather than a modifier such as "the."

Now let's look at the shape of the lines themselves. Do you want your poem to feel dense or light, fast-paced or leisurely? Line breaks can contribute to these effects, especially when the shape is paired effectively with meaning. For example:

Tense and tightly
wound, staccato

short lines strung
together without
stanza breaks
feel halting,
stagger
like ocean
chop

Whereas a poem whose lines are longer and lingering might
    suggest
Something a little more spacious, such as a curtain
breathing in and out a window or a leisurely walk
along the lacy froth of foam tracing the line
of the ocean's receding memory.

Do you see how the shapes of the stanzas mirror their meaning? Does
the first stanza look tense? Does the second stanza feel more languid
and slow moving?

These are only two possible ways to approach the shape of a poem in
a world of possibilities. The best way to experience the incredible range
of choices available to you is by studying how the poets you admire craft
their lines. Then experiment with how you use lines and white space
to sculpt your poems in the ways that feel right to you, practicing these
choices will better serve your poems over time.

- Following is an excerpt from Jane Hirshfield's poem "Lake
and Maple," presented in paragraph form without the line
breaks she has chosen.

> I want to give myself utterly as this maple
> that burned and burned for three days
> without stinting and then in two more
> dropped off every leaf; as this lake that,
> no matter what comes to its green-blue
> depths, both takes and returns it. In the
> still heart, that refuses nothing, the world

is twice-born—two earths wheeling, two heavens, two egrets reaching down into subtraction; even the fish for an instant doubled, before it is gone.

- Take this paragraph, and shape it into lines. Don't worry about right or wrong. Try to feel what shape would best embody the emotion, language, and narrative of the poem.

- Consider where you'd like the reader's eye to linger at the end of each line. On something conclusive? Intriguing? A delicious word?

- Now create a new version with a completely different approach to line breaks. If your last version had short lines, try long lines. If you ended a line with a complete idea, find a way to break it mid-thought.

- Look at both versions of the poem. Which one feels more "right" to you? Why?

- Write an angry poem. Don't say anything explicitly angry in the poem. Just try to give the reader an angry, agitated experience through the shape and momentum by using the white space of the poem. Let rage stutter through the length of the lines and the places where you break the lines.

- Find a published poem whose line breaks you admire. Write your own poem that imitates the pattern of the line lengths and the types of words at the end of each line. If the first line of the example poem is a complete sentence, yours should be, too. Where a descriptive image continues from one line to the next, yours should do the same.

ᨍ 34 ᨍ
STANZAS: THE BODY OF A POEM

A stanza is a series of lines in a poem grouped together. Some stanzas are two lines, and others are the length of an entire page or more. Some poems have a series of similar stanzas (each with four lines, for example) and others have stanzas of varying line lengths. The poet has endless choices for grouping lines into the shapes and lengths that feel right for each particular poem.

Think of stanzas as comprising the body of the poem. If a snowman were a poem, each snowball section of him would be a stanza. The size and shape of each are unique to express each individual part, yet they are also similar and related. Together, they add up to the whole snowman. In a similar way, the parts (stanzas) of a poem add up to the whole shape and continuity of the poem.

Stanzas also influence a poem's momentum. Line breaks cause the reader to linger an extra beat; the space between stanzas brings the reader to a hard stop. So, a two-line stanza will have a different impact on pacing (typically more halting) than an eight-line stanza, which allows language and images to flow a little longer without interruption. (See chapter thirty-three for more on white space and pacing.)

Unless you are writing in a specific form that dictates stanza length, such as a sonnet, how you navigate the shape and heft of your stanzas is entirely up to you. Over time, you will likely develop your own aesthetic sense of how stanzas work and what your choices mean. For example, there was a period of years when I wrote mostly in very long stanzas of uneven length. I broke the stanza when I started a new idea. More recently, I spent a few years writing poems that were primarily composed of very short, two-lined stanzas. My friend Jason declared me Queen of the Couplet. In contrast to these periods when my words and themes moved in fixed patterns, the majority of my experience writing poetry has involved trying to discover the right shape for each particular poem.

A few of my poems about disappointment in love found shape in the short-lined couplets. I felt that paired lines mirrored the yearning to partner. Clipping the lines short created for me a kind of tension, and the white space around the couplets contributed, in my mind, to the melancholy of the poem. A poem intended to be a rant or chant might have no stanza breaks and either very long lines to give a feeling of streaming momentum or very short lines to communicate intensity. And a poem about a Zen garden might have lines of precisely the same length, with four stanzas, each comprised of four lines, for balance.

Much like with line breaks, give any group of poets the same set of lines, and they will likely organize those lines into stanzas each in their own way—according to their own sense of visual aesthetic, rhythm, pacing, and meaning. The best way to find out what feels right for you is to experiment.

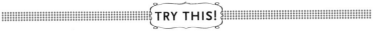

TRY THIS!

- Spend some time with a book of poetry you enjoy. Notice how many different stanza choices a single poet makes from poem to poem.

- Choose a poem of a published poet that you love. Notice how the poem's shape reflects or embodies the meaning or emotion of the poem. Notice how the stanzas visually or rhythmically appeal to you. Try to imagine how and why the poet chose to structure her stanzas this way.

- Choose a poem of your own that is of a similar line length to the published poem you've been studying. Rewrite your poem mirroring its stanza structure (number and length of lines and stanzas). Notice what you discover about your own poem as you reinvent its shape. How does a new structure impact the feeling or meaning of your poem?

- Revisit another poem you have already written and look at it with fresh eyes. Notice how the stanza breaks you chose serve or harm the poem. How might you shape the groups of lines in a way that better reflects or embodies what this poem is saying or how it feels?

CULTIVATE A WRITING RITUAL

Rituals can be useful in establishing—and sustaining—a poetic state of mind. When we train ourselves to tune into our intuition or inspiration in a certain way, we are likely to quickly enter "the zone" shortly after assuming "the position." In this chapter, we'll experiment with fun, new ways to get your creative groove on.

A ritual may be defined by time of day, the place where you choose to write (in your bedroom, on the front porch, riding the bus, at a café), the environment of that space (sounds, visual cues, lighting), the tools you use to write (notebook, computer, backs of envelopes), and even what you're drinking, eating, or wearing as you write. Your rituals will be as unique as you are.

The poet Ed Mayes says he wrote an entire book of poems, one poem a day, in the basement of his home at five A.M. every morning. First, he read a page of the dictionary out loud to get his creative gears turning, then he wrote, with great spontaneity and ease, a poem exactly the length of a single page of his small spiral notebook.

Christina Katz, the Writer Mama, says the green La-Z-Boy recliner in her childhood bedroom became a kind of magic carpet that transported her into her own, private dreamscape from which her creative writing took flight.

Rituals are not fixed; they can change over time, as we do. My first collection of poetry is divided into three sections, titled "New York," "San Francisco," and "Portland." I grouped the poems in this way to reflect three distinct chapters of my life. My writing ritual in each locale was completely different—and this significantly influenced my output.

In New York, I walked everywhere, speaking in dramatic whispers into a small, handheld tape recorder. I later transcribed my words into a document on my computer. Many of the poems born out of this ritual were fragmented explorations of the intimacies of strangers' overlapping, anonymous lives in the jumble of urban street life.

In San Francisco, I used to take a spiral-bound notebook out to music clubs, dressed in my pajamas and drinking a soda, I would listen to live music, and freewrite one thrillingly thoughtless riff until my hand gave out. The next day, I underlined the phrases that felt interesting, and typed up all the fragments. Many of them were eventually woven into poems. The resulting poems often took place in music clubs—or used musical metaphors, themes, sounds, and references.

In Portland, on my daily dog walks through the vast, misty melancholy of rainforests, I carry note cards and a pen and scribble whatever bubbles up. I also attend as many literary events as possible—and find myself overflowing with possibilities as I listen to the fine work of others. I capture every thought, with no judgment, on my note cards. I collect a little pile of these cards on my desk. Eventually, I type up my notes, and then harvest the interesting bits into poems when the time is right.

Some poets need continuity, while others need adventure and constant change. Some need noise and action around them; others need silence. What kind of writer are you?

LOCATION, LOCATION, LOCATION

Experiment with different locations and states of mind to see how each affects or influences your poetry. Try writing while:

- riding the bus
- sleep deprived
- in a friend's kitchen
- sitting in the waiting room at a veterinarian's office
- scared
- in a public restroom
- under the influence of a thunderstorm
- melancholic
- in a tent

- at a music festival
- on a diving board
- under the covers with a flashlight
- caffeinated
- sporting a cat in your lap

GOSPEL IN, GOSPEL OUT

Write for ten minutes while listening to classical music. Then write for another ten minutes under the influence of heavy metal. Try gospel, country, and hip-hop. Make sure there's some music you don't like in the mix; being a little uncomfortable can yield surprising writing. Notice how the input translates to output.

DO WHAT WORKS

As you experiment with circumstances and stimuli that benefit your writing, simply repeat what works and let go of what doesn't. If you were sitting in the bathtub in the lotus position while licking the filling of a Double Stuf Oreo when your Best Poem Ever arrived, you just might have stumbled upon the ritual that unlocks your unfettered creativity!

∽36∾
CULTIVATE A WRITING ANTI-RITUAL

*"There's a very fine line between a groove
and a rut . . ."*

—Christine Lavin

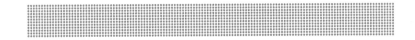

Poetry is the realm of paradox. Rituals can help poems, but they can also harm them. Having a great groove can give you a reliable point of entry. But sometimes when you get too accustomed to a certain starting place, you may find all of your poems continue and end in similar places, creating a kind of cookie-cutter effect. Or, with repetition of routine, the blade of your mind can go dull; you may risk losing the adrenaline edge that the unpredictable can bring to your life and writing.

If you've come up with a great writing ritual, good for you! Now it's time to start experimenting with an anti-ritual—not only in the ways you write, but also in the ways you live.

TRY THIS!

- Change your look. Wear your partner's or child's or friend's clothes, no matter how humorously they fit. Part your hair the opposite way. Pull out those shoes from the back of the closet that you've been too embarrassed to wear for the past decade and strap 'em on. Wear a hat or color or piece of jewelry that's *so* not you.

- Surprise yourself—and others! In second grade, I learned one of the most important lessons of my creative life from my mother when she suggested that I transform a routine book report into a sing-along. At her invitation (and with her help), I wrote my *Ramona the Brave* recap in rhyme, to the tune of "You're a Grand Old Flag." I handed out photocopied lyrics to the class, and we all sang my book report together. *Be different and be remembered,* my mother insisted. I did, and I was. How might you reinvent some routine communication in a way that has far more poetry—and staying power?

- Relocate! A change of locale can breathe fresh images, sights, smells, and dialogue into your writing. Do you usually write in a quiet room with the door closed, or a crowded café with lots of background noise? Whatever your standard venue may be, go somewhere completely unexpected—maybe even someplace you don't like—and see what happens.

- Lights out! If you write in a brightly lit room, switch to candles. If you're a mood-lighting freak, go set yourself squarely under a panel of fluorescents.

- Handwrite with your non-dominant hand. See what words are worth fighting for in a slow scrawl.

- Do the opposite of whatever you were doing whenever your last great poem came through.

- If you're a note-taker, empty your pockets or purse and walk around empty-handed. See which moments and memories follow you all the way home. And if you're far too spontaneous to keep track of your thoughts in writing throughout the day, it's time to start lugging along a notebook everywhere you go.

- Give away something that you feel you can't live without. Explore the thoughts, feelings, and language that come up as you live without it.

- Attend a service at a place of worship for a religion you've never participated in. Whether or not you believe in God, contemplate God through this lens.

- Write a love letter, apology letter, or forgiveness letter—the one that you've been avoiding since you-know-when.

- Take the long way home. Choose a route you've never tried before when traveling to a routine destination.

- Confess. Or zip those lips. Whichever is more out of character for you.

- Put on a cape and declare yourself the superhero of something: peanut butter and jelly sandwiches, dog walking, properly conjugated verbs—whatever sweet spot you are ready (or even better, not ready) to claim.

- Write a poem in which you combine two things that normally don't go together (such as poetry writing and sports broadcasting), as Jay Leeming does in his poem "Man Writes Poem" on page 120.

Shake Yourself Awake

"If you don't have a baby, have one. If you have a baby, get a sitter. If you work too much, work more. If you don't work enough, work less … If you don't drink, start. If you drink, sober up. If you're in school, drop out. If you're out of school, drop in. If you believe you have a year to live, imagine you have a hundred. If you believe you have a hundred years to live, imagine you only have one. If you're sane, go crazy. If you're crazy, snap out of it. If you've got a partner, break up. If you're single, find a lover! The shock of the new—shake yourself awake."

—Ariel Gore

Man Writes Poem | by Jay Leeming

This just in a man has begun writing a poem
in a small room in Brooklyn. His curtains
are apparently blowing in the breeze. We go now
to our man Harry on the scene, what's

the story down there Harry? "Well Chuck
he has begun the second stanza and seems
to be doing fine, he's using a blue pen, most
poets these days use blue or black ink so blue

is a fine choice. His curtains are indeed blowing
in a breeze of some kind and what's more his radiator
is 'whistling' somewhat. No metaphors have been written yet,
but I'm sure he's rummaging around down there

in the tin cans of his soul and will turn up something
for us soon. Hang on—just breaking news here Chuck,
there are 'birds singing' outside his window, and a car
with a bad muffler has just gone by. Yes . . . definitely

a confirmation on the singing birds." Excuse me Harry
but the poem seems to be taking on a very auditory quality
at this point wouldn't you say? "Yes Chuck, you're right,
but after years of experience I would hesitate to predict

exactly where this poem is going to go. Why I remember
being on the scene with Frost in '47, and with Stevens in '53,
and if there's one thing about poems these days it's that
hang on, something's happening here, he's just compared the
       curtains

to his mother, and he's described the radiator as 'Roaring deep
with the red walrus of History.' Now that's a key line,
especially appearing here, somewhat late in the poem,
when all of the similes are about to go home. In fact he seems

a bit knocked out with the effort of writing that line,
and who wouldn't be? Looks like . . . yes, he's put down his pen
and has gone to brush his teeth. Back to you Chuck." Well
thanks Harry. Wow, the life of the artist. That's it for now,

but we'll keep you informed of more details as they arise.

༺ 37 ༻
BUT WHAT DOES IT MEAN?
WHEN POEMS DON'T MAKE
LITERAL SENSE

*"It's all right to be a little lost when reading
poems ... It's not necessary to understand
everything. It's important not to lose a sense
of the unknown. Poems don't always give
themselves all at once."*

—Tess Gallagher

I used to send a poem (published by someone else) every week to a group of friends who either enjoyed poetry or wanted to get more exposure to poems. A friend's brother, a physician, opted into the list. Every week he'd e-mail me, asking me to explain the poem I'd sent.

"What the heck did the poet mean when he said XYZ? What if I'm interpreting the poem wrong? I just didn't get it. I don't want to make a mistake."

Sound familiar? Well, I'll let you in on the little insider secret that I told the physician: The poem means whatever you believe it means. I know that's not an easy answer to accept in this black-and-white world we live in, but it's the truth. Once a poet launches a poem like an arrow into the world, it belongs to the reader. While it may be interesting to speculate on what the poet intended, I think it is far more useful to consider how the poem lands with you. What does it mean and how does it feel *to you?* As a writer and reader of poetry, you've stepped into a world where anything is possible—and all interpretations are the right ones if they feel right to you.

Maybe a poem doesn't "mean" anything to you. That's okay, too. Many of the poems considered in this book are *narrative poems* that tell some kind of comprehensible story. But not all poems are make literal sense. Maybe the poem made you feel something but you don't know why. Maybe the way the poet arranged three words in a line was so surprising that it gave you a new idea for your own wordplay. Poems are often studded with surprising gifts and delights that are completely different for every reader. Regardless of what the poet may have intended, the poem becomes something uniquely yours in your hands. You and the poem make your own agreement of meaning.

Still, there will not always be something for you to love or admire in every poem you read. Sometimes a poem will offer no particular delight or revelation of any kind. This comes with the territory. Just as you probably don't like every person you've ever met, not every poem you encounter will click with you, either.

Chances are good that you will write a few poems that you don't understand yourself. For me, these poems are often born of freewriting, as described in chapter five. When the conscious mind steps aside, the subconscious often serves up some pretty interesting raw material. When I am writing a poem that doesn't make literal sense to me, I think of how Michelangelo described his process of discovering the shape of a sculpture that awaited him as he chipped away at his marble block. I believe that there is some truth that exists whole, and when I get a glimmer of such a possibility, I strive to find its shape in words. This requires a different kind of knowing and trust, like groping my way in the dark and deciding which structures feel as if they will hold my weight.

Maybe the most difficult thing about poetry is there is no definitive right and wrong way to write, and no single, universal interpretation. There is no authority beyond yourself to confirm that you have arrived and that you did it right. For example, years ago in a poetry workshop, after the poet read her poem, which took place in a bathroom, one of the students declared that the poem described a religious ritual of some kind through which the speaker was communing with God. Several students agreed. I was almost embarrassed to admit I had read the poem to describe a scary, self-hating ritual of bulimia. We were all absolutely sure of our interpretations. The poem communicated convincing meaning in two quite different directions for this particular audience. In the same vein, I have written poems that meant something very specific to me, but through writing workshops and feedback from folks who have read my book or attended my readings, I have learned that some of the poems mean something very specific to others—interpretations quite different from what I intended or could have imagined.

When writing or reading a poem, not knowing what it means is what often causes people to throw in the towel and decide poetry is too difficult. Given that most of us are socialized in an educational system that trains us to believe there is a right and wrong answer for everything, it makes sense that the open-endedness of a poem can prove challenging.

However, I propose that in the realm of poetry, the absence of an absolute is not an inevitable failure. Not knowing offers a kind of limitless potential. Poetry has taught me that life and language can be far more meaningful when we get beyond the strictures of literal meaning into the endlessly-possible place where poems live!

In the next chapter, we'll consider a number of poems that don't make literal sense, and may or may not mean something specific to you. We'll experiment with riffing on these poems to discover our own elusive truths.

38

MAD LIBS

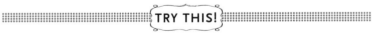

My cousin Marielle and I were on the phone when her son Shane requested an adverb that might happen in space. "Weightlessly," I proposed; Marielle repeated (and spelled) it and Shane wrote it down. This brought me back to those Mad Libs games my brother and I would passionately, competitively scrawl in the back of the car on many a family road trip. Having that built-in structure of sentences missing key words made us wild and reckless with language—like diving into the deep end, knowing we were being supervised from the side of the pool. We'd have fun startling each other with word combinations that made our sentences strangely hilarious.

I've found the same to be true with students of poetry. Inheriting the structure of an existing poem, preferably one that didn't make a whole lot of literal sense to begin with, can help you liberate your own imagination and unearth new language combinations that surprise and delight you.

TRY THIS!

Following are three poems that employ imagery and music in ways that are not confined to telling a clear, linear narrative. Notice how these poets use language. What does the skin of an orange have to do with being unmarried? How does scenery sharpen like a pencil? How does one chamomile? After fully breathing in the experience of each poem, fill in the blanks to create your own Mad Libs version. Feel free to experiment with words that feel right but don't necessarily make "sense." The trick is to find a way to get loose, without thinking too much as you write.

Jacksonville, Vermont | by Jason Shinder

Because I am not married, I have the skin of an orange

that has spent its life in the dark.
Inside the orange I am blind.

I cannot tell when a hand reaches in and breaks

the atoms of the blood. Sometimes
a blackbird will bring the wind into my hair.

Or the yellow clouds falling on the cold floor

are animals beginning to fight each other
out of their drifting misery. All the women I have known

have been ruined by fog and the deer crossing the field at night

From Inside Great Distances | by Walid Bitar

From inside great distances (don't call them dreams)
midnight is smaller than usual,
as are the ponies. Inside great distances,
unlike airplanes, are not seats
and the people far away enough
to shout to (at least the talk isn't small)
have no laps or throats when they sit beside
their donkeys and Don Quixotes, pretending
to be mirages in a cold climate. The scenery
sharpens like a pencil in my ear.
It sketches itself, and I hear of this
a bird you can color with the whites
and marbles of villas back home, bird otherwise
invisible as the price of land.
An hour, too, is invisible; why are
you feeding it at your breast, growing
it into days, months, years?

Leave it alone; visit me a little to
the North; people shave their heads
into mirrors here; I
remain (on the outside) myself.

PASTORAL | BY JENNIFER CHANG

Something in the field is
working away. Root-noise.
Twig-noise. Plant
of weak chlorophyll, no
name for it. Something
in the field has mastered
distance by living too close
to fences. Yellow fruit, has it
pit or seeds? Stalk of wither. Grass-
noise fighting weed-noise. Dirt
and chant. Something in the
field. Coreopsis. I did not mean
to say that. Yellow petal, has it
wither-gift? Has it gorgeous
rash? Leaf-loss and worried
sprout, its bursting art. Something in the. Field fallowed and
cicada. I did not mean to
say. Has it roar and bloom?
Has it road to follow? A thistle
prick, fraught burrs, such
easy attachment. Stem-
and stamen-noise. Can I lime-
flower? Can I chamomile?
Something in the field cannot.

_____ , _____ [CITY, STATE]

Because I am not _____, I have the skin of a(n) _____

that has spent its life _____ _____ _____.
Inside the _____ I am _____.

I cannot tell when a(n) _____ reaches in and _____

the atoms of the _____. Sometimes
a(n) _____ will bring the _____ into my _____.

Or the yellow _____ falling on the _____ floor

are _____ beginning to _____ each other
out of their drifting _____. All the _____ I have known

have been _____ by fog and the _____ crossing the
_____ at night.

FROM INSIDE GREAT _____

From inside great _____ (don't call them _____)
_____ is smaller than usual,
as are the _____. Inside great _____,
unlike _____, are not _____
and the people _____ _____ enough
to _____ to (at least the _____ isn't small)
have no _____ or _____ when they sit beside
their _____ and _____, pretending
to be _____ in a cold climate. The scenery
sharpens like a(n) _____ in my ear.
It _____ itself, and I hear of this

a(n) _____ you can color with the whites
and marbles of _____ back home, _____ otherwise
invisible as the price of _____.
A(n) _____, too, is invisible; why are
you feeding it at your _____, growing
it into _____?
Leave it alone; _____ me a little to
the _____; people shave their heads
into _____ here; I
remain (on the outside) _____.

PASTORAL

Something in the _____ is
_____ away. _____-noise.
_____-noise. _____
of weak _____, no
name for it. Something
in the _____ has mastered
_____ by living too close
to _____. Yellow _____, has it
_____ or _____? _____ of wither. _____-
noise fighting _____-noise. _____
and chant. Something in the
_____. Coreopsis. I did not mean
to say that. Yellow _____, has it
_____-gift? Has it gorgeous
_____? _____-loss and worried
_____, its bursting art. Some-
thing in the. _____ fallowed and
_____. I did not mean to
say. Has it roar and _____?
Has it _____ and follow? A(n) _____
prick, fraught _____, such
easy attachment. _____-
and _____-noise. Can I lime-
_____? Can I _____?
Something in the _____ cannot.

༄ 39 ༄
THE ART OF REVISION

One of the trickiest—and most liberating—aspects of poetry is that there is no gold standard against which we measure its worth. Without this standard, it can also be difficult to evaluate when a poem is finished. Because each poem is trying to accomplish something different, it is up to you to decide when the poem has arrived. This is not easy to do, even when one has been writing for decades; but it sure is satisfying to practice!

The important thing to remember about revision is that it is a process by which you become better acquainted with the poem and push it farther toward its own potential. In the revision stage, which I like to think of as Act II in the poetry drama, you revisit and may reinvent the choices you've already made with language, image, voice, music, line, rhythm, and rhyme.

The tricky balance involves wildly experimenting with what might be possible in a poem—beyond what you first laid down on the page—without losing the integrity of idea or emotion that brought you to the poem in the first place. This is a skill that develops over time, through experience and largely by feel. If it seems like you're groping around in the dark when revising, welcome to the club!

There is no fixed truth about how poems get created, or about how hard or long you should work to cross the finish line. The process is unique for each poet; and often, each poem has its own, unprecedented trajectory. I've had a few "whole cloth" poems arrive almost perfectly complete in one contiguous swoosh of pen to paper. Other poems have taken me more than fifteen years to finish. More typically, I work on a poem for a few weeks or months. Sometimes, I think a poem is finished; and years later, it proves me wrong, demanding a new final verse or line structure or title.

For the purposes of revision practice, I recommend that you divide writing and editing into two completely separate acts performed at two different sittings, preferably on different days. The goal of this checks-and-balances system is to give yourself the space to let it rip when you're writing without fear of interference from your inner editor. Don't worry: If it's bad now, it will still be bad next week; you can fix it then.

Once you feel you've exhausted every last drop of poetic possibility in the writing of the first draft, or any time you get stuck and don't know where to go next, put your poem aside for a while. The next time you return to it, you'll be wearing your editor hat. In my experience, time is the greatest editor. The longer a poem sits untouched, the more likely you are to have a sense of how to proceed when you sit down to revise.

So you're wearing your editor hat, you've rolled up your sleeves, you've checked your e-mail five hundred times, done all of the dishes, and gulped down three cups of coffee. There's nothing left to distract you; now what? The following questions can serve as a starting place for your revision regimen:

- What is most alive in your poem? Find the lines, words, phrases, stanzas that seem to be the kindling feeding the fire of this poem. Underline them so you can easily reference what's working well throughout the revision process.

- Is there exposition at the beginning or summary information at the end that is not serving the poem and could be trimmed? Often there is; experiment with cutting the first and last few lines of the poem, just to see what happens.

- Who is speaking? What would the poem be like if told from a different speaker? For example, if a poem is about an experience shared by a mother and daughter, told from the point of view of the daughter, try telling it from the point of view of the mother.

- If you are using a first-person voice, try second- or third-person. And vice versa. See how the change in intimacy and proximity influences what is being told.

- Are the similes and metaphors successful in the references they make? Could a simile be more effective as a metaphor, or vice versa? If the poem uses an extended metaphor, is it consistent throughout the poem?

- Where is language weak and flabby? How can you give it more energy and muscle? Look at each word and consider whether there's a more powerful way to convey the same thought, feeling or idea. Can passive verbs become active? Can modifiers be cut? Should "dropped" be changed to "plummeted"?

- Verb tense: What would the poem be like in a different tense than it was written? Even if it happened in the past, try the present; and vice versa. See what gives it the most power and energy.

- Does the shape of the poem (line length, stanza breaks, white space) mirror the emotion and rhythm of its content? Should it?

- Are punctuation and capitalization consistent?

- What would the poem be like with no punctuation? No capitalization? (Or the reverse, depending on your original draft.)

- Who is the audience for the poem? Is there a direct address (meaning, is the poem speaking to someone specific), and is this working?

- Is there good music of repeating sounds throughout the poem?

- Does each line break create the desired interest, pause, movement, and focus on key moments or words?

- Is the title serving the poem? Could it provide the exposition that you cut in step two, so you can move right into the meat of the matter? ("Sweetened Water Farm, 1989," for example.) Is there a key line in the poem that could be echoed in the title? How can the title take the poem further?

- Is the verb tense consistent throughout the poem? Should it be?

- Are the lines in the right order? Are they the right length for the momentum of the poem? If you're not sure, try cutting up the poem line by line or stanza by stanza and rearranging them in a completely new order multiple times until you have an "aha" moment of the perfect fit.

Concerned about editing out language you like that isn't working in a particular poem? Check out chapter seventy to learn how to manage, save, and repurpose any "darlings" that get cut throughout the revision process.

༓40༓
CONVENIENCE KILLS

I remember reading the news article about people dying from E. coli occurring in pre-washed, pre-cut, plastic-bagged spinach. At that time, I also read an interview Susie Bright conducted with a farmer who explained that spinach in and of itself is not dangerous. It is our passion for convenience—to open a bag of vegetables that someone has already cleaned and chopped for us—that requires a type of processing that makes our vegetables far more susceptible to disease.

I believe E. coli poisoning born of a desire for consumer ease is a metaphor for the endless ways we pollute our imaginations and our lives with the speed and comfort of our high-performance machinery and culture. When it comes to creativity, in many cases, convenience kills.

A few years ago, I was repeatedly caught driving under the influence of poetry (i.e., daydreaming). Rather than appreciate my alternative interpretations of the concept of "speed limit," Big Brother said, "Enough is enough." Driving 38 MPH in a 25 MPH zone four times in two years is grounds for a thirty-day license suspension. I was grounded.

It is more convenient to drive, of course, but I was curious about what life below the radar might be like. Who would I be without the privileged convenience and speed of driving I had enjoyed my entire adult life?

What I learned is that the less convenient things are, the more awake you become. On a particularly aggravating summer day of needing to be somewhere I didn't want to go, the sky was gray, the air thick and sticky. It seemed appropriate to have to physically trudge uphill, and as I set my mind and my pace to it, I stepped over a torn piece of paper on the sidewalk on 41st Avenue, probably a quarter mile or so north of my house. It looked like someone's homework. I kept walking.

After an hour's wait in an overflowing waiting room, I spent another hour walking home. This time, I slowed down over the torn page resting peacefully on the sidewalk. It was yellow, 8½" by 11", wide-ruled in blue, torn from the top out of someone's notebook. In blue pen, carefully printed in fat, bubble letters at the top of an otherwise blank page, it read: *Can't take back the things that I did before.*

I stood over this paper as if it were a baby bird that had fallen from a nest I could not find. I leapt back from it as if singed. I read it. I read it again. I looked in a wide sweep in all directions of the street: nothing. Into the heavens: no one. Who put this here? I stood over the paper for maybe another twenty seconds before some impulse came over me to grab it and fold it into my pocket stealthily, as if someone might try to tear it out of my hands.

Can't take back the things that I did before. I clutched this tattered totem of sidewalk truth in this moment of absolute, clarifying, unfathomable grace and continued walking slowly home. It lived on my bulletin board for more than a year, and in that time grew into a poem, an essay, and a philosophy about learning how to listen to what the world around us is offering. How might you keep yourself just uncomfortable and awake enough to notice the gifts that are literally falling at your feet?

TRY THIS!

- Be slow. The slow food movement and simple living movement are both centered on a basic principle: Slow down, and do what you're doing with more presence, attention, and clarity—and therefore, ultimately more pleasure. Try making a deliberate choice not to hurry through the routines and rituals of your day. See what you discover in slow motion.

- Do it the hard way. Put away that navigation system or map. Give the food processor a night off. Write a letter by hand instead of zipping off an e-mail. Move through the automated world manually for a day, a week, a month, and see what ideas and inspirations surface through these new rhythms.

- Get out of your car. If you are someone who drives everywhere, stop. For a week, find another way to get to the places you need to go. Walk, ride a bike, or take public transportation. If none of those is an option, get a ride from someone else. Even the role of passenger will completely transform a routine journey into something new.

- Spend an hour (or a day or a week) thinking and behaving like an investigative journalist or a private eye, with everything happening around you a clue. Why is the man on the sidewalk pushing an empty baby carriage? Who transformed the lawyer's office into a six-car garage, and for what purpose? Fill in your own blanks with whatever invented facts most delight you.

LET YOUR DREAMS LEAD YOU

*"The dream is a little hidden door in the
innermost and most secret recesses of the soul ...
in dreams we put on the likeness of that more
universal, truer, more eternal man dwelling
in the darkness of primordial night. There
he is still the whole, and the whole is in him,
indistinguishable from nature and bare of all
egohood. It is from these all-uniting depths that
the dream arises ..."*

—Carl Jung

Dreams travel places where our conscious minds don't. Impossible possibilities get conceived and sequenced. Metaphors rise up out of the double helix of our genetic code and echo back our ancestors, our probable pasts, our possible futures. We reinvent, recreate, and resuscitate. In dreams, anything is possible and understanding is often beyond our grasp. I think of the dreamscape as a summer field full of row upon row upon row of ripe-for-the-picking truths and metaphors and images. We can fill our buckets, stain our fingers, gorge to excess, and still there will always be more. What better raw material could a poet hope for?

Once when I was being interviewed on the radio, the host invited me to read a certain poem that she liked. This poem recounted the images and sequences of events as they occurred in a dream—worthy of a poem, in my opinion, because of its symbolic resonance. When I finished reading, the interviewer congratulated me on writing a brave poem on a topic that most women do not talk about. I don't remember what I said, but I know it was graceless and confused. I didn't understand: What was it that she thought this poem was about? I had no idea. Afterwards, a friend who had listened to the radio show called and told me how much she liked the miscarriage poem. Bingo. That must be what the radio host thought this poem was about. Maybe it is what the poem was about, though it was written years before I had any comparable life experience. I just didn't know it because the poem was writing me through its dream story.

I tell this story because I think this is a good example of the gift of the raw materials that sift through our subconscious to the surface of our waking minds. Like water lilies, our dreams are complete. They do not require our admiration or understanding to float out their impossible beauty rooted beyond our reach. Your job as a poet is to learn how to paddle out a little closer to the mysteries of your subconscious so you can get better acquainted with them.

TRY THIS!

- Keep a notebook and pen in easy reach of your bed.

- Before sleep, invite your dreams. If there is something you're curious about, something specific you want to explore, set an intention of traveling there in your sleep.

- Just as you would train yourself to respond immediately to an infant's nighttime needs, tend to your own dreams as they arise. Wake yourself up to write down the juicy stuff. It's that important.

- Don't try to force the language and images that come up into "sense." Imagine yourself tracking a wild animal. Simply follow this mysterious creature that is your subconscious and see where it leads you.

Leaving the Nest:
A Dream Sequence by Sage Cohen

I have a dream. Not a Martin Luther King kind of dream. More like a regular dream. Only bigger. One in which I know I am changing, and cannot change back. A birth dream. A death dream. A nest.

Once when I was visiting Sarah, her husband, Jason, pointed out in the lowest hanging branch of the tree beside their deck a hummingbird's nest. It was maybe twice the circumference and depth of a thimble. I watched that bird downshift from blur to stillness. Only the hummingbird's back end fit inside her little nest cup. She wore it like a hoop skirt from which her throat and head rose with a dignity of repose. I walked down the steps to stand beneath her. I could have reached up and touched her, but she knew I wouldn't. This was our agreement.

The nest has its season. Designed to be unmade and re-made with each arrival and departure, it is a far more flexible agreement with nature than the ones we humans typically make. The nest in my dream is coming undone. I walk below it, and each day it is a little less self-contained. Until yesterday, when the last scrap of fur holding things together washed away into the wet winter of my dreamscape.

Who is the hummingbird once she leaves e nest? Where does she find stillness? Authenticity is a kind of homelessness I am learning to live inside of.

∽ 42 ∾
POETRY AS TONGLEN PRACTICE

Pema Chödrön teaches tonglen practice, a style of meditation that invites us to breathe in pain—our own and the world's—and breathe out compassion for ourselves and others. The spirit of tonglen, she instructs, is to cultivate awareness that pain is not an individual burden, but rather a universal one. It invites us to let pain become a path of awakening the heart. And it calls upon us to meet and welcome our pain so that others can be free of it.

As I started breathing with intention as Chödrön instructs, it occurred to me that I already have a tonglen practice: poetry. I breathe in pain—my own and the world's—and I breathe out poems. Poetry gives suffering a direction. It uplifts our small moments to monumental ones, and gives readers an opportunity to move through pain, revelation, and catharsis with us. I have spent a lifetime seeking my own experience told more clearly in the poems of others. And I have recently released an enormous gasp of exhalation—a poetry collection—that I hope will offer readers recognition and relief as they see their own difficulties (and joys) through my eyes.

Poems may not stop the clubbing of baby seals, domestic violence, child trafficking, dog fighting, genocide, or whatever it is that feels most difficult to breathe in on any given day. But as the motorcyclist must lean into the turn to prevent a fall, poems become a kind of machinery of transport, giving you a context for leaning into the pain that you meet and safely navigating through it. My father always said, "Experience is what you get when you didn't get what you wanted." And poems are the treasures that can be exhumed from those undesirable experiences. Just think all of the great, poetic opportunities for compassion and understanding that lie coiled at the heart of every mistake, heartbreak, disappointment, and regret.

What if you were to literally look to your poetry practice as tonglen practice—a way of moving through what pierces you to the core? What injustices might it help you examine unflinchingly? What epicenter of pain or grief might it help you enter and consider? How might you relax into the universal truths of divorce, death, intolerance, and change, and make a poem offering that illumines these truths with grace?

TRY THIS!

- As you notice yourself turning away from the homeless man, the front-page news, the sobbing coming through your wall from the apartment next door, turn instead toward what is difficult. Look at, listen to, feel, and study the information communicated to you; observe how it is affecting you. What is happening? What are the specifics of this particular horror? What does it remind you of? Where do you feel this experience in your body? Where are you tight? Are you breathing? Practice inhaling deeply into your belly and relaxing your body as you continue to engage with this experience. Understand that there are people all over the world who are facing this exact same difficulty and feel the pain and discomfort that you feel.

- Write a poem for yourself, for the homeless man, for the woman whose misery is leaking through your walls. Know that in naming what you experience, you are bearing witness to another. This is a great gift of grace. Imagine that as you enter this specific pain and move through it as your write, you are making someone else's similar burden a little lighter and easier to bear.

- Share your poem with someone you know who is facing or has faced a similar difficulty. Or publish it somewhere that reaches other people who may be challenged as you are. For example, I sent a poem about a child I sponsor to the organization that facilitates my sponsorship in a Chinese

orphanage. My poem reached many people who were similarly pained—I even heard from a few of them.

- Any time you are confronted with something that feels too
  difficult to bear, return to the blank page, and write yourself
  through it.

✴ 43 ✴
I'M SO ADJECTIVE, I VERB NOUNS: ON WORD CHOICE

The title of this chapter humorously underscores the familiarity of certain grammatical patterns. We could easily plug in: I'm so hungry I could eat a house. Or: I'm so tired I could sleep on nails. (See how easily formula lends itself to cliché?) We all comply with certain patterns of speaking and writing, delineated by the rules of grammar, in order to understand each other. While this is very useful in many types of communication, poetry does not play by these rules. Instead, poetry presents us with the opportunity to discover surprising new ways to use language that circumvent familiar sentence structures—which reflect our standard ways of thinking and speaking. So let's wildly improvise until we stumble into some exciting surprises.

TRY THIS!

- Make a list of ten nouns, ten adjectives, and ten verbs that appeal to you. Maybe you like the way they sound or look, or what they mean. It may help to carry a notebook for a week or so, collecting words as they occur to you or as you experience them.

- Choose a paragraph from something in print: the newspaper, a magazine, your child's school textbook, a novel. Write it down or type it up with blanks where every noun, verb, and adjective appear in each sentence. Then rewrite the paragraph randomly plugging in nouns from your list to fill in the blanks where nouns were, adjectives for adjectives, and verbs for verbs. Don't worry about making sense. The goal here is to be spontaneously random and see what happens.

- Write a second version of this paragraph where you mix up filling in the blanks. Put a noun where a verb once was, an adjective for a noun, a verb for an adjective, adverb for a noun, and so on. Make the paragraph sound as strange and "wrong" as possible.

- Take note of all the phrases in these two experimental "poem" versions that thrill and delight you. Circle your favorites. Here's one of mine: "Let me euphony your gallant of insipidly." What does it mean? Nothing! What does it accomplish? I am thinking in new ways about how words fit together and untangling myself from the rules of grammar.

- Fill in the blanks with the most surprising words and phrases you can imagine. Don't think too hard. Just write off the top of your head and go:

  - I was too afraid to tell you _____.

  - If only the _____ would believe _____.

  - She had always wanted to _____ but _____.

  - Lately, the _____ was _____ despite the _____ it once was.

  - No two _____ will ever be _____.

- This exercise is a favorite of poet and teacher Jason Mashak. Use it to practice distilling a story to its poetic core:

  - Write a descriptive paragraph.

  - Read through it and circle the most powerful words.

  - Now rewrite using only the words circled. (How does it sound? What's gained? What's missing?)

- Add words only when completely necessary for meaning. (Of course, completely necessary is subjective. Try adding only ten words. Then cut five of them. Play with how much you can expand and contract a narrative to its essence.)

ON BECOMING REAL

*"What is REAL?" asked the Rabbit one day,
when they were lying side by side near the
nursery fender, before Nana came to tidy the
room. "Does it mean having things that buzz
inside you and a stick-out handle?"*

*"Real isn't how you are made," said the Skin
Horse. "It's a thing that happens to you. When
a child loves you for a long, long time, not just
to play with, but REALLY loves you, then you
become Real."*

"Does it hurt?" asked the Rabbit.

*"Sometimes," said the Skin Horse, for he was
always truthful. "When you are Real you don't
mind being hurt."*

*"Does it happen all at once, like being wound up,"
he asked, "or bit by bit?"*

*"It doesn't happen all at once," said the Skin
Horse. "You become. It takes a long time. That's
why it doesn't happen often to people who break
easily, or have sharp edges, or who have to be
carefully kept. Generally, by the time you are
Real, most of your hair has been loved off, and*

your eyes drop out and you get loose in your joints
and very shabby. But these things don't matter
at all, because once you are Real you can't be
ugly, except to people who don't understand."

—*The Velveteen Rabbit*
by Margery Williams

When I'm not writing poems, I'm writing marketing content; that's my day job. For the past ten-plus years, I've made my living primarily by aligning business and consumer interests through strategic communications. After a recent conversation with Noah Brier, keen observer of social and technology trends, about the potential of marketing as a peace-process intervention, I've been wondering if my poetry exists primarily as a marketing tool designed to convince me of my own legitimacy—as a person and as a writer. Because the truth is, no matter what my résumé (or my mother for that matter) may say about my accomplishments and worth, learning to believe in the Sage brand has taken nearly eighteen years of thoroughly documented reflection—the most enduring multimedia campaign of my life.

Jen Lemen, one of the leading sources of inspiration and hope in the blogosphere, made me laugh out loud when she described the extrovert's process of needing to speak everything first before writing it, which she suggested was far less efficient than the introvert's process of moving directly from thought to paper or screen. I suppose my process has been somewhat the reverse of Jen's, although I'm still not sold on its efficiencies. Most of the time, I need to write something down in order to know what I think. After I've seen the word-after-word-after-word manifest as an actual line in relationship to other lines in a poem (or essay), my thoughts find a way to establish their root system in me. Eventually, they come through in conversation.

If we are to consider our poems as our one-woman or one-man campaigns to get a little closer to who we are and what life on earth is all about, then maybe marketing and poetry aren't as disparate as I once thought they were. Both seem to be oversized mirrors that offer a way to more intimately know and reflect back the world through language.

Yet, poetry and marketing have different core objectives. Marketing is a forum for convincing and selling; poetry is a forum for exposing the bare bulb of truth. The arduous work of writing poems loves our edges off. Poems soften us into who we are and who we are becoming. They demand of us something more authentic and complete than most other experiences in life. A poem that doesn't enter the "real" space is not likely to connect with others or even resonate with the person who wrote it. Poems hold us to a higher standard by which we become more visible to ourselves and more authentic in that unveiling. It is only by writing ourselves through this poetry prism—then sharing what we've written—that we can arrive at the threadbare intimacies of "real."

❧ 45 ❧
EXPOSE YOURSELF TO ART

When I was growing up, my father had a poster that said, "Expose yourself to art." Below the headline was a photograph of a streaker opening his coat to a statue. The humor of this message made it stick; and I think of its wisdom frequently.

If you want to make art, you need to experience art—lots of it. The most important reason to do this is to shed any beliefs you might have, consciously or unconsciously, that there's only one way to write or read something. Most likely, the one way you think it's "supposed to" be done is not your way; and where do you go from there?

I attended a reading recently where several women writers performed their poems and stories. Each had a unique way of speaking her work. One was funny. One was deeply moving. One was so timid I could barely make out what she was saying. Another spoke with a rhythm and pacing that felt like ocean waves emptying themselves one on top of another on the flat mirror of beach.

At the end of the reading, a handful of us gathered to discuss what we enjoyed about the evening and congratulate the readers. Shanna, more practiced at reading her fiction publicly, wondered out loud if she had read her poem correctly. She lamented not using "that poetry voice." "You know," she said, "The one where your voice goes up an octave, followed by a dramatic pause at the end of each line." I reassured Shanna that she spoke her poems just right. Her delivery style felt natural and emotionally alive—in harmony with the content she was sharing; as a listener, I was engaged and moved.

I could relate to Shanna's concern, however. Over the years, every time I saw a reader perform his work in a way that was different from the way that I do it, I'd start to panic. After experiencing Dan Raphael's performance, where it seemed a seismic explosion of language was rising up from the core of the earth and out of him to permanently reshuffle the planetary deck, I wondered if I, too, should be pacing around the stage making dramatic gestures as if possessed by poetry. So I tried it a few times in front of my bathroom mirror and concluded: Not me.

Listening to the gorgeous, weighty resonance of Galway Kinnell's reading voice, I mourned the thin vibrato of my own. When I attended my first poetry slam at the Nuyorican Poets Cafe in New York, the loose, sexy rant-chant delivery style was so far from the more classical, stand-and-politely-read-behind-a-podium approach I was most familiar with that it woke up something in me. I started exploring ways to go deeper when reading, to make a greater emotional connection with my work and the audience. I even considered, for about five minutes, wearing leather pants as a performance prop.

While I will never read like Galway or Dan or the spoken-word woman slithering from the stage into the laps of her audience, I have catalogued all of these possibilities, and taken what was useful from each of them. The accumulated wisdom for this lifelong listener is the slow-dawning revelation that there is no right or wrong when reading poetry. Everyone delivers his work his own way—a way that's authentic for him. For most of us, it takes a long time and a lot of practice (much of which is informed by imitation) to find our way. For others, performance is an innate gift that exalts their writing effortlessly. The more you expose yourself to the art of live poetry performance, the more evident this will become.

WRITING THE LIFE POETIC

- Attend or listen to a recording of three poetry readings or slams. If you don't have access to live poetry in your community, following are three great resources for listening to poetry online:

  - Academy of American Poets—www.poets.org
  - Poetry Foundation—www.poetryfoundation.org
  - From the Fishouse—www.fishousepoems.org

  Make note of how each reader delivers her work.

- Select a poem—yours or someone else's—and imitate the style of each reader you heard as closely as possible. Read to the mirror, your dog, or a friend you trust, and observe how you sound, look, feel. Ask your friend what she noticed. Note what feels most authentic and fun for you.

  - Keep what works, and throw out the rest.
  - Repeat!

46

CREATE A SYSTEM FOR
YOUR POETRY PRACTICE

The easier it is to dive into your poetry process, the more likely you are to do it. Over the years, I have kept both paper and computer files that help me put everything I need to write or publish a poem at my fingertips. Here are some of the categories I've used. Take whatever pleases you and make it your own.

Section Name	Contents
Great Quotes	Collect quotes that move you—about writing as well as any other themes that attract you. Often a quote will suggest the beginning of a poem. Or, you may realize after writing a poem that a certain snippet of wisdom would make the perfect epigraph.
Poems I Love	I save my favorite poems by my favorite poets and refer to them often. These offer inspiration and reassurance whenever I need a refresher on what's possible in poetry.
Acorns	It's helpful to designate one, easy-to-access place where you can compile and easily reference your triggering ideas and poem snippets (see chapter sixty-two).

Poems in the Works	All draft poems that are still taking shape live here. Most of my poems spend some time ripening in this folder. When I sit down with my "editor" hat on, I generally have a selection of in-the-works poems to choose from.
Finished Poems	Keep your finished work that's ready to go public here. This will help you easily make decisions about what to send out and how to group poems when you're ready to submit to literary journals.
Contests and Publication	File submissions requirements and deadlines for contests and literary journals in one place, organized by submission date. This will help ensure that you don't miss opportunities to submit your work; you'll have the information you need to meet publications' guidelines at your fingertips.
Submission Log	Use a handwritten list, Word table or Excel spreadsheet to track when and where you submitted your work, and whether it was accepted. Make note of any personal correspondence you receive from editors so you can follow up effectively with the next submission.
Published Poems	Keep a list of your published poems and the publications in which they appear. This will help prevent mistakes, such as sending out a poem that's already been published … And it helps you keep your bio up to date with all of your latest accomplishments.
Friends' Poems	Sharing work with friends and colleagues can help inspire and motivate your own poetry practice. I like to revisit friends' writing and admire its evolution over time.

47

SPENDING MORE THAN YOU SAVE

"One of the few things I know about writing is this: spend it all, shoot it, play it, lose it, all, right away, every time. Do not hoard what seems good for a later place in the book, or for another book; give it, give it all, give it now . . . Something more will arise for later, something better. These things fill from behind, from beneath, like well water. Similarly, the impulse to keep to yourself what you have learned is not only shameful, it is destructive. Anything you do not give freely and abundantly becomes lost to you. You open your safe and find ashes."

—Annie Dillard

What would life look like if you were to write—and live—in the way that Dillard proposes? If you showed up every moment, told the truth, and risked everything, trusting that whatever was gained or lost would simply be a starting point for the next risk, the next opening, the revelation that only unfolds to those who show up and are willing? What if giving yourself freely in your writing were your only hope of survival?

It's terrifying. If you allowed your spouse, your boss, your neighbors, the people in line in front of you at Trader Joe's, to experience the full blast of who you are with no filters, you could end up jobless, homeless, and at the checkout register a little faster than you expected. Or maybe, just maybe, everything and everyone ensnared in your layered webs of "appearances" would find you even more beautiful if you showed them a little more leg, a little more complexity.

On the other hand, someone, somewhere is certain to find you hideous and leave. A question I ask myself repeatedly is: would that be so bad, in the end? Playing it safe may sustain your illusions of security. But the truth unspoken is corrosive; eventually you wake up to discover your diamonds have turned to ash—your poems the unspent seeds that never learned to blossom.

At the gym last week, I was on the treadmill next to a guy who's been a running coach at various universities. I see him there regularly; he easily muscles through several hours of running at a pop. With my head turned toward him to more easily receive his bragging, I lost my balance several times and came hilariously close to risking severe head injuries. After righting myself several times, laughing hysterically and continuing my labored beginner's jog, I told Mr. Bragging Runner that I needed to stop talking so I could maintain my balance. At which point he started making fun of me for being clumsy.

"Hey," I puffed back at him, "It's not how many times you fall down, it's how many times you get back up and keep on going that counts." That shut him up. He's a coach: how could he argue?

What if you were to start a new writing chapter and title it: "Spending More Than I Save"? What if you were to let go of more than you're holding onto, outrunning your ideas and expectations based on past experience by creating an input of new experience? What if you were to laugh uproariously at your mistakes, especially the most humiliating ones that you make over and over again? What if, each time you fell off the treadmill of your faith, you floundered around for a while, and then got right back up to try again?

A few years ago, I spent the month of January at a cabin in the country where my only source of heat was a wood stove named The Duchess. The Duchess taught me much about my craft. I discovered that writing can be a kind of catalytic converter: I feed it the raw material of my life, which it transforms into a brilliant light, a useful and enduring heat. What once may have been painful and difficult is just as nourishing as what brought me joy and ease, because to feel anything at all, to be moved to happiness or sorrow, is the thrill of being alive.

Emotion is a clean-burning fuel. I propose that you stay out of its way and let it take you wherever you are intended to go. Give it all away, and watch those diamonds glow brighter with exposure.

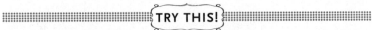

- Write your own "Spending More Than I Save" list. Brainstorm a list of ways to get outside your comfort zone and meet yourself in new ways, such as:

  - Name a treadmill or two that you've fallen off of that you're ready to climb back on and try again.

  - Do whatever makes you feel wobbly. If you sing *only* in the shower, find a karaoke bar and sign up to get on stage first. If public speaking turns your stomach inside out, go find an open mic and read something. If you're afraid of heights, find something tall to climb.

  - If there's a hobby or sport that you quit because you weren't satisfied with your performance, pick it up again and focus on staying present with the experience. Rather than judging yourself or your output, simply notice the thoughts and emotions that come up as you engage with this activity.

- Write a letter to someone in which you tell him the truth, the whole truth, and nothing but the truth about an experience that you've never disclosed to him fully (or at all). Please note that I'm not necessarily advocating sending this letter. The purpose of this exercise is to give voice to something that wants to come through simply to see how it feels and what kind of language it invites.

- Write a poem about a mistake you've made; one that still brings color to your cheeks every time you think about it; one that you'd rather no one else knew about you. Let all of the humiliation come through in your telling. Then (and this may be a stretch, but try it) rewrite the poem as if it were a great, cosmic joke; see if you can find the humor or grace that underscores your disappointment and discomfort.

♆48♆
WRITING POEMS FROM TITLES

In chapter twelve, we explored how a poem's title can float like a kite above it, adding dimension and perspective to the reader's experience. Often, a poem gets written, then titled. Or it gets titled right out of the gate and then titled again once the true direction or impulse of the poem makes itself known. In this chapter, I propose that we turn the title paradigm on its head. Let's start with a title that already exists and write a poem to match it. The title can serve as anchor, and the poem its kite flying to new and surprising heights.

Following is a list of titles by a variety of (mostly) contemporary poets. Think of this list as a book of matches: Anytime you get stuck or are unsure what to write, you can start a creative fire with a title that sparks something in you.

After you're finished writing a poem, find the original version and enjoy how your poems compare. You may be surprised at what a range of possibility a single title invites—and can accomodate!

Try writing peoms from these titles:

- "Pity the Bathtub Its Forced Embrace of the Human Form" (Matthea Harvey)

- "A Ritual to Read to Each Other" (William Stafford)

- "What Do Women Want?" (Kim Addonizio)

- "More and More I Am Vladimir" (Walid Bitar)

- "The Zero at the Bone" (Karen Holmberg)

- "Sunday Morning" (Wallace Stevens)

- "How to Listen" (Major Jackson)

- "The Jar With the Dry Rim" (Rumi)

- "Monet Refuses the Operation" (Lisa Mueller)

- "The Partial Explanation" (Charles Simic)

- "Good People" (W.S. Merwin)

- "What the Angels Left" (Marie Howe)

- "For Semra, With Martial Vigor" (Raymond Carver)

- "The Pope's Penis" (Sharon Olds)

- "The Sun Never Says" (Hafiz)

- "Poem Without You in It" (Diane Averill)

- "Give the Drummer Some" (Christopher Luna)

- "Horses and the Human Soul" (Judith Barrington)

- "Hanuman, Leap For Me" (Willa Schneberg)

- "Key to the Highway" (Mark Halliday)

- "Lyric Year" (Robin Behn)

- "The Days Run Away Like Wild Horses Over the Hills" (Charles Bukowski)

- "How the Sound of Freedom Dies" (Christina V. Pacosz)

- "Glass-Bottom Boat" (Herman Asarnow)

- "Bride and Groom Lie Hidden for Three Days" (Ted Hughes)

- "It's a Known Fact That in War" (Brittany Baldwin)

- "Gratitude to Old Teachers" (Robert Bly)

- "Snow, Aldo" (Kate DiCamillo)

- "Ladies and Gentlemen in Outer Space" (Ron Padgett)

- "The Blue Bowl" (Jane Kenyon)

- "Why Sarah Will Never Suffer Writer's Block" (Don Colburn)

- "Where No One Stays a Statue" (Mark Nepo)

- "May the Generations Die in the Right Order" (Penelope Scambly Schott)

ꙮ 49 ꙮ
CREATE A DREAM TEAM

It doesn't have to take a village to write poetry; you can certainly do it solo—and most of us do. But like so many of life's great adventures and challenges, having good company and support can make the ride far more enjoyable. I recommend the following:

WRITING BUDDY
A different kind of acceleration can happen when you work alongside someone else engaged in similar work. A regular writing date with a friend can ensure you get your butt in the chair when you say you're going to. And witnessing another poet experiencing her own writing momentum can also motivate you to work through any resistance and find your own writing rhythm.

I recommend setting and sticking to some basic ground rules, such as: Talk for ten minutes before starting and ten minutes after finishing; the rest of the time, write. Also build in time for sharing your work at the end of the writing session.

CHEERLEADER
Sometimes, all you need is to know that a poem you wrote has been read by someone who cares. For many years before I sent my poems out for publication, I sent finished poems to my friend Sebastian. She was always excited to receive my poems, and always enthusiastic about their merit. Often, she pointed out what she especially liked or thought was successful. Writing for this audience of one was thoroughly satisfying for me, because it closed the creative loop: I wrote a poem; it was read and appreciated. The exclamation point of Sebastian's participation contributed to a fragile new sense of worth—for

myself as poet, and for my poems—which, over time, blossomed into courage and confidence about my place in poetry. All that from one dedicated reader!

EDITOR

A good editor can help you see what's working well in your poetry, what your tendencies are, and where there are opportunities for improvement. If you are lucky, you know a poet or two who are a little farther along in their writing practice than you, who have a little extra time and are willing to review your poems.

I edited a few of my friend Shawn's poems recently. As we were sitting together discussing my feedback, Shawn pointed out that another poet he respected had advised him to do the exact opposite of what I was recommending. This is a great example of the value of having multiple editors. Rather than get frustrated that there is no consensus about what needs fixing in a poem, we have an opportunity to discover that there is no true right or wrong; there are only opinions. The more opinions you have, the more possibilities you may see for your poetry. And the more the "expert" recommendations conflict, the better you'll become at trusting your own instincts (see chapter sixty-four). Over time, it will get easier and easier to decide what feedback to incorporate and what to ignore.

MENTOR

One of the most valuable ways to discover what is possible in poetry is to observe firsthand someone you admire do it. Ideally, your mentor is someone you know personally, whose poetry you admire, who is willing to spend time helping you develop your own craft. But a mentor could also be a published poet, living or dead, whose poetry you study closely. Or a mentor could be a teacher, a workshop leader, or a community organizer. Anyone whose work (or whose life) awakens in you a greater sense of possibility for the poetry you write qualifies as a mentor.

50

DO WHAT YOU LOVE; THE COMMUNITY WILL FOLLOW

How does one develop a poetry dream team, you might wonder, if you're starting at ground zero? The answer is simple: Do what you love. When you're engaged with poetic events and activities in a public arena, you may be surprised how quickly you fall into step with others who share your passion. Here are some tips about how to connect with and learn from people you admire.

TAKE A CLASS

Taking a class can be the most direct way to acquire the skills or knowledge you're seeking. A class has the potential to offer both mentors and peers that benefit your writing life. More than fifteen years ago, I took an adult education poetry class at UC Berkeley. Our teacher also happened to be the editor of a prestigious local literary journal. In addition to helping me grasp some fundamentals of poetry craft and develop a critical language, he got excited about one of my poems and published it. This class gave me a sense of confidence about my work and helped me established a new sense of engagement in the wider world of poetry.

In a subsequent workshop, I met my friend Mari L'Esperance. Within a year, Mari and I were accepted to attend the same graduate program where we developed as poets together. With degrees in hand, we both returned to the San Francisco Bay Area. Back on our home turf, we continued to discuss and edit each other's poems, share the stage at various readings, and ruminate about the poetic life for nearly another decade. (We still do today—but from a greater physical distance.) I'd say I got my money's worth from that class!

GO PUBLIC

Attend readings, lectures, workshops, and other literary events in your community. When you commit to participating in the events that inspire and nourish you, the universe is far more likely to meet you halfway with interesting people and opportunities. As an example, I'll describe the connections that grew out of a single, three-day conference last summer.

At the Willamette Writers Conference in Portland, where I was teaching a poetry publishing workshop, I spent some time chatting with a lovely woman in the registration line; then we found ourselves sitting next to each other again during lunch. We exchanged cards and have kept in touch. Within weeks, both of us were accepted for representation by the same agent. Delighted by the synchronicity of our chance meeting and similar writing goals, we now write together in cafés where we discuss the writing life.

At the conference, Barnes & Noble had a bookseller table where I sold my poetry collection. During my book-signing session, I hit it off with two of the booksellers who have since become colleagues and friends. Shawn offered to host my book publication celebration at his store. Erika mentioned a desire for a poetry reading series in her store, which I volunteered to run. She took me up on my offer. With the support, encouragement and generosity of these two new allies, I've been able to further embrace and give service to the Portland poetry community—as well as develop an audience for my own work.

Not one of these opportunities was planned or expected. Every moment of good fortune was simply a result of me participating in an event that was close to my heart and meeting other people with similar passions that ultimately led to meaningful alliances.

This is how a poetic village gets built: by doing what you love, welcoming the people you meet there, exploring the opportunities to collaborate, and learning together along the way.

REACH OUT

The next time you attend a reading, lecture, or workshop, introduce yourself to the people sitting on either side of you, and learn about what brought them to this event. Approach the speaker, as well, and introduce yourself. Your support and participation is as valuable to that person as her wisdom is to you. Let that poet know what you appreciated and learned from her. Tell the people who organized the event how it benefited you. Heartfelt gratitude is a potent mortar in community building. You never know where it might lead you.

51

MEMORIZATION: BECOMING ONE WITH A POEM

"I memorized 'What the Thunder Said,' the last section of T.S. Eliot's "The Waste Land," while running around a track on the lower East Side of Manhattan. Every day, I would listen to Eliot recite the poem over and over; then, while stretching and walking home, I would practice reciting it myself. There is a section that I associate with the Williamsburg bridge, another with the smell of cut grass, one with a ship gliding by. Now when I recall the poem it brings back pieces of the environment in which it entered my soul and a certain phase in my life. The poem became, in my mind, part of my personal history."

—Nuar Alsadir

Want a great new way to show off at parties, weddings, and on first dates? Memorize a poem. It's like having a pack of tissues in your purse or pocket. You never know when having a great poem at the tip of your tongue could come in handy. It's best to be prepared.

BECOME ONE WITH A POEM

Beyond impressing your friends and loved ones with your literary prowess, memorization creates a different kind of intimacy with a poem than merely reading it. Your awareness of sound, meaning, and rhythm is dramatically heightened through the repetitive process of memorizing. You'll get inside of the poem, and it will get inside of you.

DISCOVER WHAT STICKS

More than fifteen years ago, I memorized Stanley Kunitz's poem "Touch Me," a tender love poem written to his wife of many years. That year, I also memorized maybe six other poems, but it was "Touch Me" that took up permanent residence in my mind and psyche. I think the secret to this poem's stickiness for me was twofold: it moved me deeply, and its language was visually alive. I could see and feel almost every word I was speaking; and that helped me imprint the poem such that I suspect I will be reciting it until my final days.

In contrast, despite my great admiration for Wallace Stevens's "Thirteen Ways of Looking at a Blackbird," the poem evaporated from my reserves nearly as fast as I'd memorized it. Because each section was almost its own poem, demarcated by numbers, I could not feel and retain the larger continuity of the piece. Persistent though my practice was, when it came time to recite, I'd get lost from section to section and forget what came next.

Each of us sees, hears, and conceptualizes language in a way that is unique to us. I really had no idea what poems would be ideal memorization fodder until I jumped in and started doing it. The same will be true for you. By experimenting with different types of poems written by different poets, you can discover what is most suited to become a permanent part of your repertoire. And through this process, you can perceive your own poetic tendencies a bit more clearly.

HOW TO MEMORIZE A POEM

When you set out to memorize a poem, carry a copy of the poem with you at all times so that when you have a small window of time (such as waiting in line at the post office or at the coffee shop for your morning latte), you can work on committing it to memory. I find that routine physical activity such as walking the dogs, working out at the gym, washing the dishes, and even driving (when stopped at lights) provide ideal context for engaging with and remembering language. You may have a different context or ritual that works for you.

Experiment with location, time of day, and activity until you find a good memorization rhythm. Start by reciting the first line over and over again until it comes effortlessly. Then add the next line, then the next. Always start from the beginning and speak the entire poem through as you incorporate more. Before you know it, you'll be riffing the poems you love on demand.

TRY THIS!

- Memorize three published poems that you love, one at a time. Notice which are easier and which are more challenging to retain.

- In the poems that you memorize more easily, what do you admire most about how the poets use sound, image, language, and metaphor? Since these are easy for you to remember, perhaps the poets are making choices that are akin to choices you might naturally make.

- Write a poem imitating a poem that you have memorized.

- Memorize one (or more) of your own poems.

- When you speak your poem out loud, listen as if it were written by someone else and you were experiencing it for the first time. What do you hear? What do you discover?

- Recite the poems you have memorized to a live audience, in whatever context you're most comfortable: for friends or family, or at gatherings.

༺ 52 ༻
WHO'S TALKING TO WHOM?

In every poem, there is a speaker—a person or narrator delivering the poem—and a listener—the person receiving the poem. The choice a poet makes about who's delivering the message or story, and to whom, can significantly impact the reader's experience of the poem.

For example, a poem may tell the tale of the consequences a man's addiction has had on his life. Depending on whether he's telling his Alcoholics Anonymous group from whom he'd like support, his boss from whom he'd like forgiveness, his son whom he's trying to teach not to repeat his own mistakes, or a general audience, the experience of the poem could go in a number of different directions. These possibilities assume that the man who is the subject of the poem is also the speaker of the poem, telling the story in his own voice. Another possibility is that this is a poem *about* a father, told by a narrator who is someone else: maybe his son, his boss, or his AA sponsor.

All of this is to say that any given poem could be approached from a range of vantage points. (For more on point of view, see chapter fifteen.) As the writer of the poem, it may behoove you to experiment a bit with a few different ways into any given poem to learn how you want to tell it and how you'd like your reader to hear it. For example, do you want the reader to know from an objective distance that the young lover is anguished with heartbreak? Or do you want to stand your reader in the wobbly shoes of the accused ex who has just emptied every drawer and bank account? Each engages the reader differently and gives him a different vantage point from which he participates.

TRY THIS!

- Take a poem you've already written and tell it differently. Let's say it's a poem about a particular experience you had, told in an omniscient voice to no one in particular. To create a new slant, you might revise this poem to tell a first-person story to a specific listener—perhaps the person who carried you out of the schoolyard that afternoon—or the person who you wish had done so.

- Experiment with how a speaker's gender, age, and temperament might alter the experience of a poem.

    - Write a nature scene, perhaps about a snowstorm, in the voice of a child—from her point of view.

    - Write about that same scene from the point of view and in the voice of the snowman she's built.

    - Now let the cedar tree standing tall above the scene narrate from its lofty vantage point.

    - Let the reader see this scene through the eyes of the guy who drives around plowing snow on his day off.

- Now reinvent the poems by writing *about* a child in a snowstorm, the snowman she's built, the lofty cedar tree, and the guy driving the plow.

- The following poem is told in the first person, in the voice of the painter Max Beckmann, addressing a specific you (this is called a direct address)—a person who also appears in his self-portrait. (From the series "Self Portraits" after paintings by Max Beckmann.)

Nagoone Berries | by Sage Cohen

The thorn bush holds her secrets
low to the ground.
In the privacy of rain
we kneel together,
heads bent to the berries.
Lush with leaf and hush
our voices settle like fog
among the unspoken
as we stain and bruise ourselves
with fruit. The earth drinks
and drinks until it spills open
and raw like a prayer book saturated
with God's desire for humanity.
We are a rhythm of choosing, crawling
along the bloated field through
necklaces of vine. The berries fall
wide-eyed into our collecting cup.
You carry that tender burden
of severed fruit home.
You stand over the stove,
cooking sacrifice
down to sugar.

Consider how this poem might have had a different impact if it
were delivered from a different point of view. For example, how
would you receive it if there were no direct address—if instead,
the "you" were replaced with "he"? How might this narrative
be told if the narrator were omniscient (with "we" becoming
"they")? Try rewriting the poem using one of these approaches.

ᴗ53ᴗ
LECTIO DIVINA:
THE ANCIENT ART OF
READING AND LISTENING

When I learned from my friend Martha how her church group was reading poetry together, I became very excited. Borrowing from the ancient art of Lectio Divina (Latin for "divine reading"), a Christian tradition involving a slow, deep listening into the Scriptures, the group created a ritualistic space for delving deep into poems. I propose you do the same.

Following is an adaptation of the five steps of Lectio Divina designed to guide you in developing a contemplative poetry reading practice. Gather with a friend or a group and bring enough copies of the poems you want to study for everyone to read (and write on). Find a comfortable, quiet place to sit where you are all in easy view and earshot of each other. Time each step to suit the group's comfort level and attention span.

THE FIVE STEPS OF LECTIO DIVINA*

1. **Read.** Designate a facilitator who reads the poem aloud without others seeing it, then distributes the poem for others to read.

2. **Ruminate.** Read the poem aloud to yourself, equipped with a pen. As you read and reread the poem, make notes in the margins and on the poem itself. As you write, feel free to:

---

* Thanks to Louann Reid who adapted (and has graciously agreed to share here) the process of Lectio Divina described by Jon Knapp for her class "Approaching God Through Poetry."

- Ask questions.

- Make observations.

- Highlight or underline words and phrases that strike you.

- Note connections or associations that the words have for you.

- Identify a word or phrase that really speaks to you; you may have a reason, but you don't have to.

3. **Mediate.** Through discussion, everyone in the group shares his questions, observations, associations, and favorite phrases. In this step, everyone strives to get closer to the meanings a poem holds for each person and the group. Anyone can comment at any time, and group members should feel free to answer the question or respond to the comment. The designated facilitator takes notes and consolidates the group's exploration to capture the shared discoveries of meaning and appreciation. Whatever the group concludes through mediation is not fixed in stone. It's just a starting place for each member's ongoing mediation of poems.

4. **Celebrate.** In this step, the focus is on meditation and contemplation, with a goal of discovering new ways to consider the poem, and therefore "hear" what it has to say to you. Much like a Quaker reading, people are invited to read "as the spirit moves you." I recommend proceeding as follows:

- Choose a phrase that appeals to you and repeat it to yourself so often that it's almost memorized.

- One person begins by saying her phrase. When you hear a phrase that seems to somehow relate to yours (or as the spirit moves you), say the phrase you have chosen.

- Continue saying words and phrases from the poem as long as anyone wants to continue.

- The most important part of this step is listening. Listen carefully to what the poet has to say and to how other members of the group have found meaning in the poet's words.

- Notice how the celebrations of others inform your own appreciation of the poem. As you read it again, do you discover a new insight, or language you appreciate, that you hadn't noticed before?

5. **Reflect.** Spend a few minutes in silent reflection. Does it seem that there is an invitation in this poem? Are you called to do anything? How does this call—if there is one—relate to your appreciation of your own life, your comprehension of the human condition, or your place in this world? You may want to write some notes to yourself, or just reflect in silence.

〜54〜
MIXING MEDIA:
THE WORLD AS YOUR CANVAS

Andy Goldsworthy, a British sculptor, photographer, and environmentalist, composes art out of natural and found objects. In *Rivers and Tides*, the documentary about his work, we witness the artist spending days composing painstaking sculptures of twigs, rocks, leaves, flowers, icicles, mud, thorns, and snow. Nearly as soon as these masterpieces are finished—and often before—they are unmade by an alchemy of natural forces such as wind, rain, currents of large bodies of water, and time. This film impressed upon me the transience of art in general and our limited capacity to imprint our world.

Striking a similar chord of reverence for transience, Natalie Goldberg, one of the most well-known freewriting gurus, recommends not only writing down our spontaneous thoughts and language, but also speaking them out loud. Rather than regarding each thought as a precious commodity that must be preserved, this spoken-word approach seems to invite the opposite: that we practice turning the tap of our creative faucet on at will and cultivate a trust that there will always be more flowing through when invited.

Both Goldsworthy's and Goldberg's approaches to making art seem to pay homage to process as much as (if not more than) product. They have invited me to consider that the experience of crafting something may be far more satisfying than actually crossing the finish line of completion. Somewhere between finishing and preserving, what is most alive in the creative process goes dormant.

This chapter is about waking yourself up to the fun of generating language, for no purpose other than to delight in its trajectory through you. Here, you're not trying to impress anyone, win any contests, garner praise, or pat yourself on the back. You're not concerned with pinning down the wings of those fleeting moments of genius. It's time to don your "Poets just want to have fun" t-shirt and look to the world as your creative oyster.

A notebook is good. Your computer is fine. But what if you expanded the canvas of how and where you wrote your poems? What if you were to experiment with writing on new surfaces, using materials you've never considered? What types of poems would emerge on each? Would a napkin invite a rumpled, tangential poem? Would a poem written in chalk in your driveway discuss the transience of humanity? What would you write in permanent marker on something that would get you in trouble? What would you have to say in the space of a steamy bathroom mirror?

TRY THIS!

- Write on index cards. (What thoughts, feelings, and images are sustained in small spaces?)

- Say it in watercolor with big, fat, purple, juicy words.

- Fogged windshields and bathroom mirrors are ideal places for capturing a melancholy moment.

- Write a love letter on parchment paper with a fountain pen. Burn the edges.

- What do your unfinished pancakes have to say? Write in whipped cream or syrup on your plate.

- Tell your dog.

- With a stick in sand, write words of impermanence.

- Cover your bedroom wall or living room floor with rolled-out newsprint. Write big and small, in zigzags and circles. Welcome the thought or poem or story that has been waiting to emerge in such spaciousness.

- Spray paint it on an interior wall of your house.

- Write it in chalk on a playground.

- Put a message in a bottle and send it out to sea.

- Pass a handwritten note to someone under her desk.

- Write it on a receipt.

- Say it underwater.

- Make a banner and hang it over your front door.

- Squirt it in dish soap on your pots.

- Make your own fortune cookie fortune.

- Write it on someone's cast or pant leg or t-shirt.

- Write a postage-stamp-size message on a Post-it note!

- Say it on the surfaces of leaves and the petals of flowers.

- Stitch it in needlepoint.

- Speak it out loud, into the wind.

- Write a press release.

- Post it in a blog—your own or someone else's.

- What clumsy messages might want to come through your non-dominant hand? Or a poem penned by your toes?

❦ 55 ❦

THE ART OF "ALL DAY"

"People don't have time management issues;
they have determination issues."

—Christina Katz

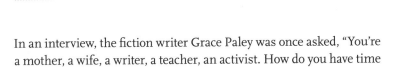

In an interview, the fiction writer Grace Paley was once asked, "You're a mother, a wife, a writer, a teacher, an activist. How do you have time to do it all?" To which Grace responded, "Well, I have all day." This little snippet of dialogue has come to represent what an entire month's worth of silence taught me.

A few years ago, I had an experience that turned my sense of time inside out. I spent the month of January at Soapstone, a writing retreat for women on the Oregon coast. My days at Soapstone were a rhythm of nothing and everything: hauling wood in a wheelbarrow, maintaining the wood stove, cooking and eating, reading, writing, and sleeping. Outside the daily press of deadlines and traffic, to-do lists and to-call lists, I got wet (it poured daily). I got quiet. I became green with breathed-in earth and trees. Sleeping beside the raging creek, the container of self I arrived within was shaken loose, broken open.

On the writing retreat, I retrained myself to the truth that spaciousness is a choice. With twenty-six consecutive "all days" that belonged to me, I started to wonder: What am I so busy doing all day at home that I (think I) don't have time to read, don't have time to talk to my neighbors, don't have time to really focus on petting my cat when he makes a spontaneous appearance in my lap? It became difficult to remember what's so much more important than being present in my life. I understood for the first time that I have all day every day, if that's how I choose to live it.

Have a "cup is overflowing" day. Instead on focusing on the time you don't have to write, turn your attention to every little scrap of time you do have. With ten minutes in a doctor's waiting room, fifteen minutes on the train to work, a half hour on the elliptical machine at the gym, practice attuning yourself to a poetic state of mind.

Have a notebook on hand or a copy of the poem you're memorizing or a few index cards to capture that wispy, diaphanous phrase as it drifts across the big sky of your mind. As you become practiced at these short, creative stints, you may be surprised at how much writing time you are able to carve out of your jam-packed days.

Create a writing retreat. Once you've mastered sprinting in small creative spaces, you're ready to start stretching for an occasional marathon. Designate an uninterruptible chunk of writing time: the most time you can possibly afford. Go anywhere outside of your daily routine where you feel comfortable and able to focus. Whether you travel to the café around the corner for two hours or to a tropical island for a week, it is important that you have a feeling of oasis where you are not tempted to talk, twitter, e-mail, web surf, or in any other way distract yourself from the delight of sinking in to a spacious writing time that belongs only to you.

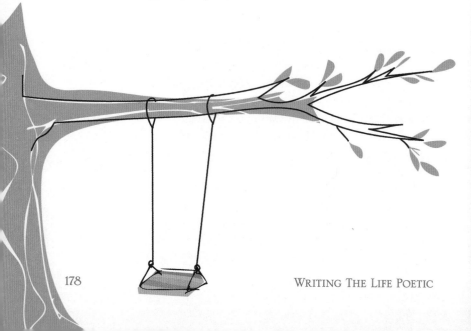

WRITING THE LIFE POETIC

Reprioritize. When I was single, I spent most nights out seeing friends or attending literary and musical events. When my fiancé moved in and I started writing two books on top of a full-time job, I suddenly had to make different choices about how to spend my after-work hours. With some time and retraining, I scaled back my social life as I kicked my writing (and my relationship) into high gear.

When you're clear about your priorities, your choices are likely to reflect what you value. Try living a week as if writing poetry were your number one priority. Who could you skip talking to on the phone? What TV show could you pass on until next week? What fat might be trimmed from your days in service to your lean, mean writing machine?

Write graffiti. Because I am highly suggestible, I write myself notes showcasing whatever propaganda I'm selling myself at the moment, and post them prominently. "You have all day!" sits over my computer like a good idea I can always count on; I use it to remind myself that I will have enough time if I make enough time for what matters. Write down a phrase that helps you feel more spacious about time, and experiment with using it to keep yourself motivated.

✾56✾
BE SLOW

You can't rush a flower bud to open; it blossoms in its own time. Likewise, a poem happens in poem time. What's tricky is that there is no fixed or predictable pattern to poem time. One poem may come flying into your field of vision completely formed like a bride's bouquet tossed to you. And the next may take shape only after you crawl on your hands and knees through garden after garden searching for just the right heft and fragrance of blossoms. A century plant blooms once in its lifetime—this can take twenty-five years; I just finished a poem I started in 1995.

When Mary Oliver was asked at a recent reading why she didn't teach or read publicly until she was in her sixties, her response was simple and instructive: "Because I hadn't found my voice yet and I wasn't ready." If Mary Oliver, winner of the Pulitzer Prize, was willing to write herself ripe before going public, I propose that the rest of us might consider taking a deep breath, relaxing our shoulders against the backs of our chairs and doing the same.

In today's über-speed, instant-gratification world of text messaging and e-mail, poetry offers an alternative path: a slow one. Poetry has taught me a great respect for slowness. It is one of the only things I have been willing to wait for, work at, wait some more, and keep on working. I recently heard Ira Glass advise an audience: If you really want to do something well, you have to be willing to do it really badly for a very long time. Like Glass's passion for broadcast storytelling, my love for poetry has always been blind; I believe in the potential of each poem and remain undeterred by repeated failures to achieve that potential. Through this pursuit of potential, I have labored and loved words into greater and greater alignment over the course of more than twenty years. And I expect to be staggering uphill, anguished with the delight of love and tickle of imperfection for the rest of my writing life.

TRY THIS!

- Do you commute somewhere regularly by car, bus, or train? If so, choose a routine route—to work, school, carpool, or the grocery store and do as follows:

  - Notice your surroundings as you travel. Write down the details of what you see, hear, and smell along the way.

  - Now try that same route, or part of it, on a bicycle, if you can. When you return home, write down all of your observations.

  - Traverse your route a third time, this time on foot. Write down your observations.

  - Compare the three versions of your observations. How do they compare? Where does the most interesting detail come in? On which version of the journey did you feel most tuned in to the world around you and your place in it?

- Is there something you already do that you've been willing to do badly for a long time? (Training my five-year-old German Shepard mix dog would go on my list here!)

  - What have you learned from this process? How has it shaped you? Strengthened you? (I've learned that repetition is the best and only way to learn something completely.)

  - How might you apply what you learned in this other area of your life to poetry? (I try to come back to the same unruly poem again and again with the patience and daily discipline of repetition that I channeled for two years while teaching my dog not to chase the cats.)

- Write a first draft of a poem, and set a goal of finishing it in three months. Sit down with the poem once a week at a set time until you feel finished for the moment. Then put it away and don't look at it again until the next week. Notice how you feel about the poem and the writing process along the way. How does this writing compare to poems that you have written at other speeds and time intervals?

ᴗ 57 ᴗ
ART IMITATES ART

Certainly, art imitates life. And life, in many ways, has come to imitate art. A third variable to consider when writing poems is the tradition of art imitating art. Perhaps you've heard Don McLean's song, "Vincent (Starry, Starry Night)" about Vincent van Gogh, or seen the movie *Girl With a Pearl Earring*, which tells the story behind the famed painting of the same name by Johannes Vermeer. Wallace Stevens's poem "The Man with the Blue Guitar," is said to be written in response to a statement Picasso made about his theory of painting. You might have your own personal references and examples of art's influence on art. Why not integrate this into your own poetry practice?

If you haven't yet tried writing poems about paintings, songs, sculpture, dance, or other poems, you might want to give it a go. Sometimes, inhabiting another artist's state of mind or aesthetic can give you a visual, auditory, or linguistic starting place that is far from any you might have chosen yourself. Like being out in a small boat in unknown waters, you'll learn quite a bit from rowing yourself back to shore. In the process you may unearth new sensibilities and strengths, and an expanded sense of your own style.

TRY THIS!

- Visit a museum. Find a painting you like and write from inside it, as if you were the naked woman carrying the basket or the melting watch draped across the landscape. Or, as Paulann Petersen does in the example on page 186, explore the implications of a color. Consider what it may mean to the story of the painting—or how it may influence your experience of it.

- Attend a ballet or symphony performance. Write a poem that is not *about* what you experienced, but one that strives to capture and convey the experience itself. Relax and imagine that you *are* the dance or the musical composition, and notice what language moves through you.

- Just as Frank O'Hara contemplates the virtues of his craft compared to the craft of his painter friend in the poem on page 185, make a date with an artist friend (one who practices a craft that you have no experience with) and inquire about her creative process. How are ideas born, developed, revised, and ultimately presented in this other creative endeavor? What can you learn from this process and apply to your own writing?

- Write a poem about a poet you admire but do not know. Imagine the circumstances that informed the writing of a particular poem of his. Imagine the childhood experiences or temperament that have shaped this poet's aesthetic or reputation. Why was Sylvia Plath depressed? Why does Jack Gilbert stay so far out of the limelight?

- Write a poem about writing a poem—or about reading one.

Why I Am Not a Painter | by Frank O'Hara

I am not a painter, I am a poet.
Why? I think I would rather be
a painter, but I am not. Well,

for instance, Mike Goldberg
is starting a painting. I drop in.
"Sit down and have a drink" he
says. I drink; we drink. I look
up. "You have SARDINES in it."
"Yes, it needed something there."
"Oh." I go and the days go by
and I drop in again. The painting
is going on, and I go, and the days
go by. I drop in. The painting is
finished. "Where's SARDINES?"
All that's left is just
letters, "It was too much," Mike says.

But me? One day I am thinking of
a color: orange. I write a line
about orange. Pretty soon it is a
whole page of words, not lines.
Then another page. There should be
so much more, not of orange, of
words, of how terrible orange is
and life. Days go by. It is even in
prose, I am a real poet. My poem
is finished and I haven't mentioned
orange yet. It's twelve poems, I call
it ORANGES. And one day in a gallery
I see Mike's painting, called SARDINES.

CIRCUS | BY PAULANN PETERSEN
AFTER CHAGALL

Begin with a red fan
open in the bareback rider's hand.
I understand red. I know how it leaps
from her fingertips to the dress
pouring down the horse's grey side.
I see this fan and this dress,
how they ignore her pale breasts,
pretending to notice only her lips
and the flower sipping fire in her hair.

Red mouths the gossip
from her lips to the man's,
words that seem to disappear
into his shirt's dark sleeve
but are really caught in deep gathers
of her skirt. I know this fanfare,
trumpets starting a show
red began long ago.

〜58〜
WRITING THE ZEITGEIST

"Trust me on this one. Americans don't want to know how to die. They want to know how to lose weight. How to get rich. How to sustain that erection! Be the poet of erectile dysfunction, and you might just be the poet who can afford to pick up the check."

—Michael Lewis

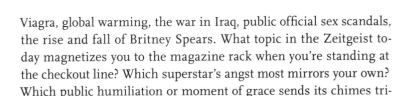

Viagra, global warming, the war in Iraq, public official sex scandals, the rise and fall of Britney Spears. What topic in the Zeitgeist today magnetizes you to the magazine rack when you're standing at the checkout line? Which superstar's angst most mirrors your own? Which public humiliation or moment of grace sends its chimes trifling down your spine? What news item lines up with what you believe or fear or hope?

The news covers the so-called objective truth about the issues, people, and events that we all share through the one-way lens of our media portals. What might your poetry have to add to the conversation about our cultural icons, blasphemies, and rejoicings? Check out how these poets have responded to the spirit—and events—of our time with their own voices, interpretations, wisdom, and humanity.

LORENA | BY LUCILLE CLIFTON

it lay in my palm soft and trembled
as a new bird and i thought about
authority and how it always insisted
on itself, how it was master
of the man, how it measured him, never
was ignored or denied, and how it promised
there would be sweetness if it was obeyed
just like the saints do, like the angels
and i opened the window and held out my
uncupped hand; i swear to god
i thought it could fly

ASPHODEL, THAT GREENY FLOWER (EXCERPT) | BY WILLIAM CARLOS WILLIAMS

It is difficult
to get the news from poems,
yet men die miserably every day
for lack
of what is found there.

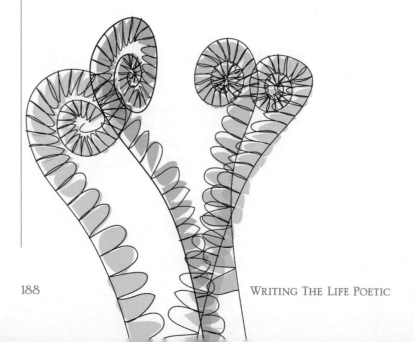

CHER | BY DORIANNE LAUX

I wanted to be Cher, tall
as a glass of iced tea,
her bony shoulders draped
with a curtain of dark hair
that plunged straight down,
the cut tips brushing
her non-existent butt.
I wanted to wear a lantern
for a hat, a cabbage, a piñata
and walk in thigh-high boots
with six-inch heels that buttoned
up the back. I wanted her
rouged cheekbones and her
throaty panache, her voice
of gravel and clover, the hokum
of her clothes: black fishnet
and pink pom-poms, frilled
halter tops, fringed bells
and that thin strip of waist
with the bullet hole navel.
Cher standing with her skinny arm
slung around Sonny's thick neck,
posing in front of the Eiffel Tower,
The Leaning Tower of Pisa,
The Great Wall of China,
The Crumbling Pyramids, smiling
for the camera with her crooked
teeth, hit-and-miss beauty, the sun
bouncing off the bump on her nose.
Give me back the old Cher,
the gangly, imperfect girl
before the shaving knife
took her, before they shoved
pillows in her tits, injected
the lumpy gel into her lips.

I wanted to be, stalwart
and silly, smart as her lion
tamer's whip, my body a torch
stretched along the length
of the polished piano, legs
bent at the knee, hair cascading
down over Sonny's blunt fingers
as he pummeled the keys,
singing in a sloppy alto
the oldest, saddest songs.

AT THE BOMB TESTING SITE | BY WILLIAM STAFFORD

At noon in the desert a panting lizard
waited for history, its elbows tense,
watching the curve of a particular road
as if something might happen.

It was looking for something farther off
than people could see, an important scene
acted in stone for little selves
at the flute end of consequences.

There was just a continent without much on it
under a sky that never cared less.
Ready for a change, the elbows waited.
The hands gripped hard on the desert.

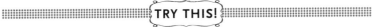

- Write about a story you heard in the news from the inside out, by either inhabiting the point of view of someone or something in the story. Do not describe how you feel about these events. Let the details you choose illuminate the emotion. Look to Lucille Clifton's "lorena" as an example.

- Visit Poets Against War (www.poetsagainstthewar.org) and read their "Poems of the Month." Write a poem that describes your own thoughts, experiences with, or beliefs about war. If it is a thematic fit, consider submitting your own poem to this site for publication.

- Choose a famous person you've always emulated or despised, as Dorianne Laux does in "Cher" on page 189. Write about what is most intriguing to you about that person. What does he represent to you? What have you learned about yourself by studying this person?

- Write a poem that takes a position: in favor of a political candidate, a local, national or international policy, a religious doctrine—whatever you feel most passionate about today.

Tell Someone Else's Story

*"The poet enjoys the incomparable privilege
of being able to be himself and others, as
he wishes."*

—Charles Baudelaire

*"Whenever I attempt persona poems, I do so
with a tremendous amount of humility. Any
attempt to adapt another's perspective and
imagine the impact of his or her experiences is
about empathy—about wanting to understand
something [that] sits at a distance from my
own direct experience. It also provides an
opportunity to look back at myself and the
conditions characterizing and extending from
my own life through different eyes. Ideally, such
an endeavor requires something to change or
take root as a result. If I've succeeded at writing
an effective persona poem, I am not quite the
same person I was at the outset."*

—Tracy Smith

Many people think of the poem as a soapbox of personal confession.
But your poems don't have to be about you at all—at least not directly.
What if you could be anyone in a poem? Whose story would be most
fun—or strange, or scary—to tell?

The English language gives us first person singular (*I*) and first person plural (*we*). Poetry gives us "first person universal," a way of tapping into the universal human experience by exploring and inhabiting it through a first-person narrative. You are not limited to your own personal experience and knowledge in poetry. You can be anyone, anywhere, at any time in history—past, present, or future. You could even write a poem describing what Darth Vader sees from the chamber of his dark helmet. Darth Vader is a fictional character—one that may in no way resemble your own life. This does not exclude you from imagining and writing from within his experience, if you're moved to do so.

A persona poem is a poem written in the first person, in which a writer imagines she is someone or something that she is not: an animal, a historical figure, an object. The Greek word *persona* means "mask." The persona poem offers a unique opportunity to mask your own point of view and look at the world through someone else's eyes. You may find a new kind of freedom to say things you might not otherwise say, or explore experiences that are otherwise out of reach. Persona poems can be playful or serious. It's really up to you.

I stumbled upon the persona poem completely by accident in my college creative writing class when the professor played us a recorded version of "Amazing Grace," and we were invited to write a poem in response. Listening to that powerful anthem used in the Civil Rights Movement transported me to another place and time, and I found myself writing a poem about Rosa Parks.

As I wrote, I became Rosa on that day in 1955 when she refused to give her seat to a white passenger. With pen to paper and "Amazing Grace" raising the hairs on my arms, my tongue thick with fear, every cell in my body tensed with clarity of purpose. I saw the jiggling overhang of the bus driver's stomach as he stood up and moved toward me, pasty face flushed with rage. The stifling weight of every passenger's eyes bore down on me as I held my head erect, eyes private and proud ... In the writing of that poem, for just a moment, I penetrated history.

Maybe you've always wondered why Grumpy of the Seven Dwarfs is so grumpy. Or what really happened with that cigar in the Oval Office.

Choose a speaker. Whose story do you most want to tell? Remember, you are not limited to "real" people. Mr. Spock, Zeus, The Cat in the Hat, and a jar of applesauce may all qualify.

- What happens in the poem? Select an event or story to tell. Whether it is ordinary or extraordinary, know why you chose to portray this moment in time.

- Date yourself. Is your poem happening in 2009 or during the Middle Ages?

- Consider word choice. The poem's diction or word choice should reflect who the speaker is and where he is in time. For example, Marie Antoinette's language is likely to sound very different from Porky Pig's.

- Describe the setting. Details bring any story to life. Show the reader the environment through specific, detailed description to give him an opportunity to enter the poem.

- Put your title to work. How concisely (and intriguingly) can you tell us who the poem is about, who is speaking, who they are speaking to, and what the central conflict is?

- You are about to tell a story that has never been told before. Enjoy the ride!

～60～
THE ALCHEMY OF DOING NOTHING

I am a doer. I'll bet I have more action items on my to-do list than Imelda Marcos has shoes. Sometimes I wonder if my relationship with this list is akin to Sisyphus's regard for his boulder. I am ever striving to get across that illusory finish line where I just know I'll stumble upon all of the lounging people who are certain that they've done enough.

I had an experience years ago in San Francisco that challenged this accomplishment mania at its core. It was the height of the dot-com boom, and everyone on the planet had decided that San Francisco was the In Place to live. Rents were outrageous, and vacancies were minimal. This was the time that I brilliantly brought an unplanned puppy into a "no dogs" apartment from which I was promptly evicted. Desperate to find an affordable place to live that would accept me with my two cats and puppy, I spent every waking moment searching online, calling property management firms, and frantically driving—with the endless throngs of other desperate people—from open house to open house. I was getting nowhere.

One day, my friend Sanford suggested, "What do you think might happen if you just did nothing for a while?" I looked at him as if he had just proposed that I cut off my right leg. What kind of person would do nothing when something needed to be done right away?

With venom in my voice, I replied, "I know what would happen if I did nothing." (dramatic pause) "Nothing!" But I was wrong.

The next day I got sick, and then sicker. My search came to a screeching halt; I had no choice. I had to stop striving.

Lo and behold, within forty-eight hours, Sanford stumbled upon a For Rent sign in his neighborhood on his way to the café. He drove me there to look and when we arrived I sat stunned in the car; this was the biggest, loveliest space with the cheapest rent that I'd encountered in my entire citywide search. Sneezing and sniveling, I went in to speak to the property owner who happened to be there sorting through a pile of maybe forty applications. Within ten minutes, she tossed the applications aside and said, "I know I'm not supposed to make decisions this way, but I like you, and this place is yours."

From this experience I learned that stillness can be as useful as action when it comes to getting important things done. The road can only rise to meet you if it knows where to find you.

What if doing nothing was simply more productive than doing something? What if that poem you are writing and rewriting with mounting frustration needs to simply settle for a while so its ingredients can get acquainted, then rise like dough in its own time? If you let yourself be empty, what alchemy of inspiration or truth might you stumble upon as you sit with your discomfort of not knowing? Nature has its time of growth and expansion, its time of harvest, and its time of rest. Poetry should, too.

TRY THIS!

- The next time you're stuck, struggling, or can't figure out what to do with a poem, consider taking a nap, going on a hike, doing yoga, cooking, or gardening. Doing physical work or play can help loosen the mental knots that get tangled up when writing.

- Put that unfinished poem in a folder titled "To Revise" and don't look at it for at least a week.

- Spend a day on the couch in pajamas with no commitments. Read, eat, listen to, and watch whatever pleases you most.

- Cultivate your poetic compost by taking a class in something creatively engaging but unrelated to poetry, such as: improvisation, flower arranging, percussion, watercolor.

61

WRITING VOICE

Anyone familiar with the poems of Charles Bukowski and Emily Dickinson could easily distinguish one poet's work from the other. Identification is possible because, over time, poets develop a sensibility that is expressed in their style, themes, linguistics, images, and music. This unique expression is a poet's *voice*. Just like fingerprints, no two poetic voices are the same. This is what can be so liberating and frustrating about writing poetry.

There was a time that I considered throwing in the towel when it became clear that I would never write exactly like Sharon Olds, then Frank O'Hara, then Nuar Alsadir. What I didn't understand then was that not writing like these poets would afford me a richer and more surprising journey: learning to write like me! In the end, my repeated attempts to imitate these poets' voices helped my own strengths and sensibilities find their footing without too much self-consciousness. This is why I think imitation is so valuable: It keeps you so focused on another poet that you don't trip over your own feet quite as much. Equally important, it gives you valuable examples of what is possible in poetry. (For more insistence on the importance of imitation, see chapter twenty-seven.)

The moment of greatest despair, when you finally accept that you will never be the next Blake, Rukeyser, Kenyon, or García Lorca, is also the moment of greatest potential. Chances are good that in this moment, you've stumbled upon some way of being, seeing, writing that is yours and yours alone. Don't worry too much about feelings of competition or futility that may come up along the way. Think of them as fuel for the journey. Let them pique your curiosity about how to enter a poem and travel within it. Let them invite you into your human vulnerability: one of the richest sources of poetic potential.

Poets commonly talk about searching for—or finding—their voice. I equate this with searching for your shoe size. The shoe size is already there, even though you may need to try on any number of different shoes to discover what it is. Voice is not something you need to pursue. You already have it. And paradoxically, the more you apply yourself to the study, admiration, and imitation of other poets' voices, the more effectively you'll be nurturing your own.

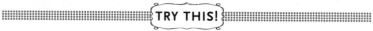 **TRY THIS!**

- Spend some time reading the work of a poet you admire. Read at least ten poems to get a representative feel of his work—the more the better.

  - Write down three qualities of the poet's voice that you notice. (Is she particularly apt at metaphors? Do her poems happen in nature, in domestic scenes, or in imaginary places? Do her poems have a music that invites you to speak them out loud? Is there a certain feeling she typically conveys or a mood he creates?)

  - Choose two other poets for the next two days and repeat.

  - Once you feel very familiar with all three poets, make a few notes comparing how their voices differ, and how each one is uniquely identifiable to you.

Writing The Life Poetic

- From the list of voice attributes that you've compiled, choose the three that appeal to you most. Focus on introducing these one at a time into your own poetry. Strive to imitate the approach each poet took in his poems.

- Come back to your poems a few days later. Notice if you've made any choices that seem surprising to you. (Such as: I didn't know I could write a powerful metaphor. Or: I always write about nature, and in this poem, I wrote explicitly about myself. Or: I am starting to experience language as a kind of music.)

- For each poet whose voice you imitated, write down the ways in which your own poetic voice is most like and unlike his.

- Return to this chapter every time you're feeling discouraged by another poet's prowess and your feelings of relative lack of worth.

62

SAVE ACORNS: KEEPING TRACK OF YOUR GREAT IDEAS

What happens when you sit down to write and no bolt of lightning strikes you? When it comes to inspiration, I say there's no offense like a great defense. Squirrels use their feasts to prepare for the famine, and so can you. When your mind is alert to the acorns of inspiration—and you have a good system for saving those acorns—you can build up a surplus. This secret stash of great ideas can keep the pilot light of inspiration going, and get you through the harshest winters of creative dormancy. Following are suggestions for catching, sorting, and saving inspiration. Experiment with whatever appeals to you, and create your own acorn rituals.

CAPTURING INFORMATION ON-THE-FLY

Your daily life is brimming with raw material. Here are some ways to catch and keep it until you're ready to write from them.

- **Post-it notes.** My computer screen is littered with paper and virtual Post-it notes. When sitting at my desk doing other work, this is the fastest, easiest way to capture a poetic thought the moment it arrives. By strategically placing Post-it note pads where you're likely to need them most, you can ensure that every good idea that flits through is assured a safe landing.

- **Index cards.** One of my favorite systems for capturing acorns is via 3" by 5" index cards, which I have at my side at all times. They're in my purse, in my car, in my dog-walking shoulder bag, on my desk, and next to my bed. That way, when inspiration strikes, I can get the idea down fast and then move on with whatever I'm doing. Index cards are light, easy to transport, and disposable as soon as I've transferred a good idea to one of my idea-saving systems.

- **Notebooks.** Kim Stafford, the person who taught me this fabulous acorn metaphor, carries a beautiful, handmade (by him) notebook in his pocket at all times; he records his acorns there. A notebook or notepad can be a receptacle in which to capture, save, and admire acorns over a period of time. Each collection becomes its own masterpiece of possibility—so you can see what you were thinking during that period of time.

- **Recording devices.** Not everyone enjoys or has the time to capture his moments of fleeting genius in writing. Also, for people who are more verbal than visual, speaking poetry might feel like a better fit than writing it down. Sometimes it is best to have both options. I have had contexts where writing was preferable, and others where voice recordings worked better, depending on my mode of transportation, ability to have hands free, etc. Carrying a small, lightweight voice recording device can be a great way for you to capture the poetry of your life moment by moment.

CULLING, SORTING, AND ORGANIZING ACORNS

Once you've scribbled down the fragment of overheard dialogue or captured that moment of grace before it melted away like a snowflake, what do you do with it next? Here are some tips for preserving your great ideas until you're ready to use them.

- **Tubs, baskets, and bins.** Create an acorn holding bin where you can deposit your Post-it notes, index cards, cassettes, and notebooks until you're ready to use them. My friend Christina Katz uses project-specific plastic tubs for collecting ideas and inspiration. I have a few wicker and cloth bins that I use to store stuff for creative projects. The next time you decide to write a poem and don't know where to begin, you can cull through your acorn bin as though you're on a treasure hunt.

- **Bulletin boards and whiteboards.** Sometimes it helps to have your ideas right in front of you, in your line of sight, to keep you on track, or to see how a concept is developing. Post them on a bulletin board or write them on dry-erase whiteboards. I like to collect quotes and inspiration on my bulletin board; on the whiteboard I write my latest goals and aspirations.

- **Paper file folders.** If you have a file drawer or a metal stand, paper files can be a simple solution for collecting loose acorn scraps in a way that's easy to access.

- **Computer files.** I have a single document in my computer titled "Acorns" into which I enter in consecutive order all of my scribbled-on-paper ideas. After a handful of index cards and sticky notes collects on my desk, I transcribe these into the acorn document, date each entry, and then recycle the paper. I like having this ever-expanding record of my creative process at my fingertips when my inspiration well is running dry. At the very least, it reminds me that at one time in recent history I did have an interesting idea!

Once you start experimenting with acorns, you'll find a system of recording and retrieving your ideas that works for you. You may be surprised at how much inspiration your mind serves up once it knows that you're paying attention.

ᨳ 63 ᨳ
TAKING SHAPE: EXPERIMENTING WITH POETIC FORMS

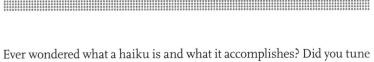

Ever wondered what a haiku is and what it accomplishes? Did you tune out when your high school teacher incanted your first Shakespeare sonnet? Do villanelles, pantoums, and sestinas sound like planets from some far away galaxy? Traditional poetic forms bring an enforced structure that sometimes includes specific rhythms, rhyme patterns, and syllable counts. While writing within the confines of these various forms, I've always stumbled upon ideas and language I probably would not have otherwise written. The challenge of "making it fit" seems to stir up its own kind of magic.

Following are some basic maps that chart the pattern of a few poetic forms, as well as examples that bring the patterns to life. Employ these in your own writing to discover what themes await you in each form you choose.

HAIKU
Haiku is a Japanese form that typically explores the natural world, the human condition, and the relationship between the two using simple language that does not rhyme. All haiku have three short lines; the most common form has the following syllable counts (although exceptions, like the example on the next page, are common):

> Line 1: five syllables
> Line 2: seven syllables
> Line 3: five syllables

UNTITLED | BY ISSA, TRANSLATED BY JANE HIRSHFIELD

On a branch
floating downriver,
a cricket, singing.

PANTOUM

The pantoum is a form originating in France in which lines repeat
from stanza to stanza, creating a kind of echo that can carry emotional
topics well. In this form, lines 2 and 4 in each stanza become lines 1
and 3 in the next. This pattern repeats throughout all stanzas—typically at least five to seven. In the final stanza, line 3 from the first
stanza becomes lines 2; line 1 from the first stanza becomes line 4 to
bring the poem full circle. This pattern is detailed below, then brought
to life with an example.

Line 1
Line 2
Line 3
Line 4

Line 2 repeats
Line 5
Line 4 repeats
Line 6

Line 5 repeats
Line 7
Line 6 repeats
Line 8

Line 7 repeats
Line 9
Line 8 repeats
Line 10

Line 9 repeats
Line 1
Line 10 repeats
Line 3

Pantoum of the Blind
Cambodian Women | by Mari L'Esperance

Years later my mind returns to them
Their sightlessness a physical mystery
Blindness a deliverance from memory
Eyes darkened in mute refusal

Their sightlessness a physical mystery
As if it were all that was left to them
Eyes darkened in mute refusal
It is this that has kept them alive

As if it were all that was left to them
The women have turned inside themselves
It is this that has kept them alive
Through the burning, falling world

The women have turned inside themselves
There is no returning, the boats departed
Through the burning, falling world
Their vision turned inward to the bearable

There is no returning, the boats departed
Forced to watch their daughters bayoneted
Their vision turned inward to the bearable
This is the story of their turning away

Forced to watch their daughters bayoneted
Blindness a deliverance from memory
This is the story of their turning away
Years later my mind returns to them.

SONNET

Sonnets, first written in Italian as love poems, were made popular in England by Shakespeare. The first half of a sonnet typically presents a theme or raises an issue or problem. The second half of the poem addresses this problem, with a significant change (called a turn) toward the last two lines. Following is the rhyme format for an English (Shakespearian) sonnet:

Line 1: a
Line 2: b
Line 3: a
Line 4: b
Line 5: c
Line 6: d
Line 7: c
Line 8: d
Line 9: e
Line 10: f
Line 11: e
Line 12: f
Line 13: g
Line 14: g

SONNET 116 | BY WILLIAM SHAKESPEARE

Let me not to the marriage of true minds
Admit impediments. Love is not love
Which alters when it alteration finds,
Or bends with the remover to remove:
O no! it is an ever-fixed mark
That looks on tempests and is never shaken;
It is the star to every wandering bark,
Whose worth's unknown, although his height be taken.
Love's not Time's fool, though rosy lips and cheeks
Within his bending sickle's compass come:
Love alters not with his brief hours and weeks,
But bears it out even to the edge of doom.

If this be error and upon me proved,
I never writ, nor no man ever loved.

MORE ABOUT FORMS

If you would like to learn about poetic forms (such as villanelles, sestinas and others mentioned here) in far more detail than this chapter can cover, I recommend checking out one of these books:

- *The Making of a Poem: A Norton Anthology of Poetic Forms* edited by Mark Strand and Eavan Boland

- *Poetic Meter and Poetic Form* by Paul Fussel

- *The Teachers and Writers Handbook of Poetic Forms* edited by Ron Padgett

‿‿64‿‿
TRUST YOUR INSTINCTS

"There is an unseen life that dreams us; it knows
out true direction and destiny. We can trust
ourselves more than we realize, and we need
have no fear of change."

—John O'Donohue

One of my students was stranded between the points of view of two experts. She sent me an e-mail spelling out her dilemma. First, she heard Edward Hirsch speak about the importance of the poet's relationship with his reader. Then, a few weeks later, she read Li-Young Lee's contemplation of the mystical connection between the poet and the poem, in which there is no mention of the reader's experience as an end goal. The student wasn't sure how to integrate these two different points of view into her own writing. Is the poet ultimately responsible to the poem or to the reader? How do you balance the reader's needs with the poet's needs to commune with her poem?

I assured her that this kind of dilemma is exactly where students of poetry want to be: in between ideas that don't agree. There is no single right way to do anything in poetry. There's only what's right for each poet. The more points of view you can expose yourself to, the more likely it is that you will find something that feels like the right fit for you.

For example, I recently read Ted Kooser's insistence that a poem must be written to say something clear and specific to the person on the listening end. I happen to disagree with this. My own personal belief is that poems have something to say, period—some of which may be easily decipherable by the reader and some of which may not be. If I had read Kooser's advice and nothing else in my formative writing years, I may have edited out a dimension of my writing that has been the most instructive to me over the years.

Every poet has her own motivation for writing and philosophy about writing that informs her unique process. Your job as a poet is to become your own expert and clarify for yourself why you write and what you believe about writing. As master of the one-of-a-kind instrument that is you, you will learn to play it in the way only you can. This kind of wisdom is not arrived at by sitting around and thinking about poetry. You learn who you are by observing what you do. The more you write poems, the better you'll know what advice to take and what advice to ignore.

So listen to all the experts—the more the merrier—and test out every single theory and hypothesis for yourself. Are you writing strictly toward the pleasure of connecting with an audience? Great! Go for it! Are you writing for the mystical journey of communing with your poem? That's an important thing to know about your process so you can honor it.

As you seek guidance, keep your eyes and ears trained to what expands your sense of possibility for your writing; and do what you can to tune out any advice that feels limiting. Remember, you are seeking insight that can help you do what you're doing better—not to be told that what you're doing is not allowed.

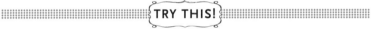

- As you attend lectures and readings, write down the gems of advice that poets offer about their own process and philosophy.

- Seek out essays, interviews, and recordings of poets in literary journals, anthologies, video and audio archives, and online. Listen to what they say about how and why they write. Make note of their techniques and approaches.

- Create a document that you can update to help you track how the advice of the experts lines up with what you're learning about poetry. Here's how mine might begin:

Name of Poet	Poet Believes	I Believe
Ted Kooser	The poem must speak clearly and audibly to an audience.	The poem must say what it's meant to say—whether that's meaningful to a wide audience or not.

- Over time, you're likely to have a number of entries for certain poets. Take note of which poets' suggestions really click for you. For example, I find Tess Gallagher's and Jane Hirshfield's writings on poetry give me a greater sense of expansiveness and possibility for my own.

- Seek out more wisdom from the poets who really resonate with you.

- Every now and then, revisit your "I believe" list to see if your sense of your writing—or what's possible in poetry—has changed any over time.

Remember: Exposing yourself to the insights of other poets can help you learn to trust *your* instincts better.

ᘯ65ᘰ
BE ANONYMOUS

I still remember the thrill I felt nearly fifteen years ago when I first stepped up out of the subway darkness into the mid-afternoon glare of Times Square in Manhattan. I had just flown in from San Francisco and was on a quest to find a place to live in New York City, where my graduate program would start the next month.

As I squinted in the daylight, looking for street signs to orient me, I was jostled off balance by a sea of strangers rippling around me. In the pointillism picture of this moment, I was a mere speck. Surprisingly, this sense of being swallowed up into the vastness of NYC was exhilarating to me. My first thought was, "No one knows me here. I could be anyone, do anything." There was something absolutely liberating in the anonymity of being a person who didn't belong in a new place.

I've had this same feeling while traveling in a number of other places, domestic and international: squished among strangers riding public transportation in my own town and trekking by backpack in other countries. When we travel, there is a certain distance from the identities we wear at home, at work, in our communities. We are not in a proscribed environment, and therefore our responses are not proscribed. With a bit of distance from the thesis statements of our lives, we may feel freer to move around in the margins of mystery. This departure from routine can be a godsend for the writing mind.

In my late twenties, before leaving my home in California for a trip to a remote coastal town in Mexico, I wrote on a Post-it note, "Find Eliza," and stuck it to my computer screen. Eliza was my college roommate with whom I had fallen out of touch over the years. I was pretty sure she was still living in the same city that I was, and I intended to look her up when I got home. As it turned out, I didn't need to wait that long. Eliza was staying in the room next door at the tiny little traveler's lodge in Puerto Angel, Mexico. I emerged from a nap one afternoon to find her swinging in the hammock, chatting with my boyfriend. This is a good example of how the unpredictable nature of travel can make it a little easier to find yourself strangely surprised, synchronistic, and alive.

Since travel is not on everyone's to-do list, nor in everyone's budget, let's explore ways you can extrapolate the freedoms and anonymity of such journeys to your everyday life.

TRY THIS!

- Shake up your daily rituals so you experience new places and people.

  - Buy coffee at a different coffee shop; pretend you are your best friend Bob, and say to the barista what Bob might say.

  - Jog a different loop than you're in the habit of running, and pay attention to what you notice about the people and scenery in this new locale.

  - Take a bus or train during rush hour to somewhere you don't usually go. Or take the route you're accustomed to, but get off at a different stop.

- Participate in something local that exposes you to throngs of people: a shopping mall on a weekend, a music concert, a ball game, or a marathon. Take a few notes about what you observe and feel surrounded by strangers. How does anonymity register for you?

- Attend a community meeting that you've never participated in before, a PTA meeting, a religious group, or a political organization. If you prefer to sit in the back row, choose a seat right in front of the podium. If you are shy, make an effort to channel your bossy older sister and see what it's like to be outspoken for an hour. If you're the life of the party, see what it's like to sit back and listen. Notice how people respond to you—or don't—in this new role.

FIND THE RIGHT HOME
FOR YOUR POETRY

*"Online journals are certainly as legitimate as
print journals. Indeed, because of their real-time
and increasingly interactive nature, they may be
more legitimate."*

—Simmons B. Buntin

When you're ready to go public with your work, you have a range of
options. Following is an overview of the various types of publications
and venues you might consider exploring.

PRINT JOURNALS

Print literary journals are the classic and most respected venue for publishing poetry. These publications typically include a mix of poetry and
fiction—and sometimes essays, photos, and artwork as well. Payment
for publication in literary magazines is uncommon; instead, it is typical to receive a copy or two of the journal in which your work appears.

The standard reference for researching potential markets for your
poetry is *Poet's Market*, published by Writer's Digest. Listings here
are coded so you can easily search for the right fit for your skill level,
publication history, writing style, and subject matter. Other useful
resources include:

- Duotrope's Digest (www.duotrope.com)
- The Poetry Market E-Zine (www.thepoetrymarket.com)
- *The International Directory of Little Magazines & Small Presses*

ONLINE PUBLICATIONS

Online journals are becoming increasingly popular places to publish and read poetry. According to Simmons B. Buntin, response and publication times often are shorter than print journal turnaround time. Plus, with a greater number and variety of online journals (many of which are themed or topical), you have a greater chance of seeing your work accepted and published. Check out a few:

- Arch Literary Journal (www.artsci.wustl.edu/~archword/)
- convergence (www.convergence-journal.com)
- diode poetry journal (www.doidepoetry.com)
- No Tell Motel (www.notellmotel.org)
- Paradigm (www.paradigmjournal.com)
- Slow Trains (www.slowtrains.com)

A quick online search will help you identify a wide range of additional online journals. The ones you enjoy reading are the ones to which you should consider submitting your work.

CONTESTS

Contests are a great way to get visibility and money for your poetry. Often, contest winners are rewarded with both publication and a cash prize. Most contests require a submission fee—around ten to twenty dollars is common—and these can add up, so be thoughtful about how frequently and where you submit your work.

Here are a few reliable resources for learning about contests:

- Absolute Write (www.absolutewrite.com)
- Funds for Writers (www.fundsforwriters.com)
- Poets & Writers (www.pw.org)
- Erika Dreifus, The Practicing Writer (www.practicing-writer.com)
- Winning Writers (www.winningwriters.com)

A note of caution: There are presses and organizations that offer contests where, unbeknownst to those who participate, everyone who enters wins something. All winning poems are then published in a large volume, and winners are encouraged to buy these collections for seventy-five dollars or more. Such presses are called vanity presses, because they prey on the vanity and naïveté of poets who do not have enough experience to know this is not a legitimate publishing venue. You should never have to pay to receive a copy of your published poetry. Any publication that requires you to do so should raise a red flag; investigate carefully before proceeding.

CHAPBOOKS

Chapbooks, mini poetry books comprising anywhere from five to fifty poems, are a great first step in the book-publishing journey. The most typical route to publishing a chapbook is by submitting it to chapbook contests. (You can learn about these contests through the resources listed on page 214.) You can also submit directly to a publisher, but this will take more research and planning. Self-publishing—another way to go if you don't want to play the submit-and-wait game—is steadily gaining in popularity and acceptance. If you're concerned that publishing a chapbook could interfere with publishing a larger volume later using the same poems, don't be! Chapbooks give you legitimacy—not to mention confidence—and can even help you publish a book (using some of the same poems) later.

POETRY BOOKS

Poets typically consider publishing a book once they have sixty or more finished poems, and are more likely to be considered seriously by publishers once fifteen to twenty of those poems have been published in journals. Much like the chapbook publishing process described above, contests are the most typical route to book publication; and self-publishing is an increasingly popular alternative.

If you'd like to self-publish with minimal out-of-pocket expense, consider print on demand (POD) publishing with a vendor such as Lulu (www.lulu.com). You simply post a formatted manuscript online, and a book gets printed each time someone purchases it. Keep in mind that once you self-publish a collection of poetry, the same rules apply as if it were published by a poetry press. You will no longer be able to submit the individual poems in that collection for contests or publication; nor will you be able to publish the collection with another publisher in the future.

How to Submit Poems
for Publication

*"If you have no credentials, just put in a cover
letter saying, 'I appreciate your considering
these new poems for Magazine X.' But if you've
been published, listing the three or four strongest
publications is a good idea, as it shows others
have validated your work before."*

—Jane Hirshfield

Once you've taken your time writing and polishing your poems, then
waited as long as possible to let the poems—and your stomach—settle,
you may be ready to submit your poems for publication.

All you need to start sending out your work is a group of three to
five poems that feel finished. However, to give yourself a good buffer
of trust in your own writing machismo and momentum, I recommend that you wait until you have at least twenty polished poems
before you start sending them out. That way, should you find yourself
in a crisis of faith about any one poem, you have a whole stable of
others to fall back on.

Submissions by mail typically include: three to five poems (this
may vary per submission guidelines), a cover letter, and a self-ad-
dressed, stamped envelope (SASE). The publication will use the SASE
to return your poems to you. Online submissions, which are becoming increasingly popular, may have a field for entering biographical
and previous publication information. E-mail is the typical means of
notification for online submissions.

The following rules of thumb will give you the best chances of making a favorable impression when you submit poetry to journals for consideration:

1. **Don't ever send your work to a publication that is unfamiliar to you.** You should have read at least a few issues of your target journal, and have a sense that your work is similar to the type of work it has previously published, or fits with its aesthetic. You also want to confirm that the quality of poetry is such that you'd be proud to have your poems published in its pages.

2. **Create a great cover letter.** An effective cover letter is short and sweet. It should name the contest or issue for which you would like to be considered, if applicable, and name the poems you are submitting. A brief biographical statement should mention any relevant publishing, teaching, or community-building credentials. Make it clear that you have read and are familiar with the publication. Most importantly, be gracious.

3. **Avoid simultaneous submissions.** Most literary journals do not appreciate poets sending the same poems to multiple publications for consideration at the same time. You can send unique sets of poems—with no overlaps—to different journals simultaneously. Let's say you have twenty finished poems; you could send groups of five (different) poems out to four different publications all at once.

4. **Before submitting to a publication, always read and follow submission guidelines.** These can be found at the publication's Web site, or in *Poet's Market* or *The International Directory of Little Magazines & Small Presses*. The submission guidelines should provide any important deadlines, formatting requirements, and other key submission preferences. For example, some magazines require you to include your name and contact information on each poem. And others (typically for a contest where poems are read "blind") will

disqualify any poem with contact information on it. This is also where a publication will specify its simultaneous submission preferences.

5. **Be professional**. Proofread your poems and cover letter as carefully as you would a résumé for a new job. Type each poem on its own page, and print it out on clean, white paper. Taking your poetry seriously will encourage those on the receiving end to do the same.

6. **If a poem is two pages or longer**, make sure you include the poem's title and page number at the top of subsequent pages, as well as a note indicating whether this page begins with the "same stanza" or a "new stanza" from the previous page. Note that unless you are submitting to a publication that focuses on long poems (more than two typed pages), your chances of publishing a one-page poem are better because most publications don't have the space to dedicate to long poems.

7. **Expect to wait.** The realm of poetry publishing is about as far from instant gratification as you're likely to get in this day and age; be prepared to wait at least a few months for a response to your submission. And if your work is accepted, it may be at least a few more months before it goes to print. (Response and publication times for online submissions are usually faster.)

THREE STEPS TO POETRY PUBLICATION

Taking the first step toward publishing can be the hardest. Equipped with this simple formula, you'll have a process you can repeat again and again to find the right home for your work:

1. Look at the "Acknowledgments" page of a contemporary poet's book whose writing feels similar to your own. Write down seven literary journals where the poems in this book first appeared.

2. Go to a bookstore or library to read those seven journals. (Some might have their content available on their Web sites.) Choose the three journals that feel like a fit for your writing. You may also refer to a resource such as *Poet's Market* to learn more about each publication.

3. Send your strongest three poems to the first journal. (Make sure you follow their submission requirements.) If the poems are not accepted, send them to the second journal. And then the third.

An aside for the faint of heart: Think of this process as practice, and don't worry yet about the results. You are establishing a poetry publishing habit that can last a lifetime, and this is just the beginning.

⚘68⚘
Blogging as Beginner's Practice

A blog (or Web log) is a special kind of Web site that is easier to update and less expensive to maintain than a traditional Web site. Blogs consist of a series of entries or posts that users can publish online almost instantaneously. Many blogs are updated regularly—often daily.

Poets and writers typically use blogs to share their own work, resources, inspiration, and thoughts about the writing and publishing process. Many include art, photos, podcasts, and videos. Following are a few of my favorites, each with a unique approach to the literary life online:

- mole (http://koshtra.blogspot.com/)
- jenlemen.com (http://jenlemen.com/blog/)
- Year of the Books (http://yearofthebooks.wordpress.com/)

Unlike traditional publishing, a blog gives writers the ability to publish their own work at little or no cost. And unlike print journals, books, and anthologies that offer no feedback loop, most blogs include a "comments" feature, which allows readers to respond to posts. This can result in the development of communities and dialogues involving people from all over the world.

WHY BLOG

- **Create accountability.** For a beginning poet, a blog can be a great tool for developing your writing practice. I started blogging in 2006 (www.sagesaidso.typepad.com) because I wanted to challenge myself to write something new every day. And for nearly a year, I did just that. Though I didn't tell anyone about my blog, the possibility that someone might stumble upon it gave me a little extra motivation to polish my work before saving and publishing it online. In effect, the blog helped me become more accountable to my own goals, while also establishing a sense of accountability to my potential readers.

- **Measure your progress over time.** Blogs appear as a series of posts that scroll, with the most recent posts at the top and the oldest at the bottom. Historical writing is archived by month. This gives you an easy way to archive your work and observe the evolution of your writing over time. Plus, looking back at six months' worth of daily or weekly poems can give you a great sense of appreciation for your commitment to your craft.

- **Build community.** Blogs can be a great way to connect with other people who are new to poetry. Through the comments function you can cheer each other on, share ideas, and learn and grow from an interactive peer community.

HOW TO GET STARTED

You can literally start blogging in a matter of minutes. All you need to do is choose a blog host, sign up, and go! Check out these four popular blog hosts and see which one feels right—and most affordable—to you. (Some are free, and most are low cost.)

- TypePad (www.typepad.com)
- WordPress (www.wordpress.com)
- Blogger (www.blogger.com)
- LiveJournal (www.livejournal.com)

You may also want to cruise around the blogosphere and see who's using which host. This may help you decide what feels like the right home for your blog.

- Create a blog.

- Every day, or at whatever interval is reasonable for you, do a single "Try This!" exercise from this book and post it on your blog.

- When you have fifteen entries under your belt, give yourself a pat on the back and then up the ante. Maybe you can challenge yourself to write more often, or include more finished poems in the mix. Maybe you want to write a little blurb about a reading you attended in your community or a new literary journal you just discovered. See how you can stretch and expand your sense of what it means to write a poetry blog.

- Invite a friend or a few friends to read your blog. Notice how your writing and feelings about writing change when you know you have readers.

- When you're ready, send an e-mail to sage@writingthelifepoetic.com and tell me your blog's URL. I'll post it on the Writing the Life Poetic blog (www.writingthelifepoetic.typepad.com) along with other readers' blog information. Reading and learning from peers can give you new ideas, inspiration and energy for your own work.

Blogging to Build an Audience

If you are new to writing poetry or sharing it publicly, chapter sixty-eight will give you everything you need to know about blogging for the next few years at least. However, if you have an established writing practice and are already comfortable sharing poems with a wider audience—or if you're blogging already—you may be ready to start approaching your blog with a little more strategy.

WHAT A BLOG CAN DO FOR YOU

For the intermediate and advanced writer of poetry, a blog can be a great way to gain a virtual foothold by increasing your visibility, confidence, poetic prowess, and community.

- **Increase visibility.** With every blog posting, your name, poems, themes, and subject matter become increasingly more visible to those doing online searches. Over time, you will develop a substantial trail of virtual crumbs leading folks to your virtual blog door.

- **See your writing more clearly.** There's nothing like having an instant, interactive audience to give you greater insight into what you're writing. Once you start blogging regularly, you'll learn from the people who participate in your blog via the "comments" function what's useful, engaging, and controversial to a wider audience.

  For example, you may think that your great strength is the music of your language. However, you may hear from readers that your imagery is what really grabs them. Or maybe you'll learn that folks think of you as the poet who writes about eggs, horses, heartbreak, or whatever your recurring themes may be. I thought my blog was entirely "literary" until I attracted an audience of readers whose blogs were all "spiritual." There's nothing like a feedback loop to help you better understand the impact of your poetry. Their comments gave me a more comprehensive perspective on my own work.

- **Hone your craft.** When you write a poem that then sits in a drawer or file cabinet or on your computer hard drive, there may be no fire burning under you to refine and improve it. Whereas, when you know that a real, live reader—maybe many readers—will be reading what you write when it goes live on your blog, this is likely to keep you striving for excellence.

- **Build your platform!** In the world of publishing today, blogging can be a key component in generating buzz. A blog is a great way to expand your audience, reinforce your poetic prowess, and prove to editors and publishers that you are a serious, working poet! (To learn more about how a marketing platform can help lead to a book deal—and how to create one, check out Christina Katz's *Get Known Before the Book Deal: Use Your Personal Strengths to Grow an Author Platform*.)

TRY THIS!

- Check out the blogs of the poets listed at the Writing the Life Poetic blog (www.writingthelifepoetic.typepad.com).

- Find three blogs you like, and leave comments for the poets describing what you appreciate about a certain post or their blog in general. Visit and comment as often as time and interest allow. Participating in the blogs of others increases your online visibility and helps you establish relationships with peers. It's not uncommon for authors and readers of a blog to check out your blog after reading your comments.

- Link to the poetry blogs that you like in your blogroll—which is a listing of links to your favorite Web sites and blogs. This is good for you and good for the blog you're linking to; it increases traffic both ways.

- Use tags in each blog post to indicate the themes or subjects covered in that post. This will increase searchability and visibility for your blog.

- Think of your blog as a one-person literary journal. What types of information do you want to include that will engage you and your readers? Explore ways to vary the content to keep folks coming back for more. Reblogging (writing an overview of an interesting article or blog post and linking to it) can be a fast and easy way to offer something of value without having to create it from scratch every time.

- Have fun! Think of your blog as your virtual muse. Use it to challenge and inspire yourself to discover new subject matter, new inspiration, and new poetry friends out there in the blogosphere and beyond.

70

DARLINGS: REPURPOSING THE SLUSH PILE

Like anything worth doing, poetry is a long-term commitment. The bad news, for all of us socialized in an instant-gratification culture, is that there is no shortcut to percolating your poetic prowess. The good news is that there is not a single scrap of thought or language that is ever wasted along the way. Everything you write helps you know your mind more intimately and hone your agility with language. In my experience with poetry, there is no such thing as wrong or lost . . . only a continuous trajectory of moving toward. And you're always getting closer.

A common mistake poets make is keeping language in a poem because they are attached to it, despite the fact that it may not be serving the poem well. Just because a word or phrase or idea isn't working in one poem doesn't mean it won't be perfect in another. Often, you may be working with similar ideas or themes over a period of time, and language excerpted from one piece can be the perfect starting point (or finishing flourish) for something else.

When I extract something that isn't working in a poem, I simply save it somewhere easily accessible for future use. I call these little displaced gems my "darlings" and save them in a cumulative document titled "Darlings" on my computer. I can quickly and easily dip into this resource whenever I'm culling the dregs of my thinking for fresh material.

Within this larger context of developing yourself as a poet over time, darlings can let the steam out of the pressure cooker of your writing process. Rather than get tangled up in forcing solutions out of language that's not working, you can put aside what is worth preserving for later, and keep your attention trained to what is working today.

Save up for a rainy day. When cutting language you like from a poem in the works, keep a "darlings" folder, document, or notebook in which you retain those moments of genius that haven't yet found their appropriate context.

Keep inspiration close at hand. Store your "darlings" resource somewhere handy so that you have your own vault of linguistic gems at your fingertips the next time you need it.

Visit your darlings often. Each time you begin a new poem, or find yourself stalled in the middle of one, scan through your "darlings" repository to see if any language pops out at you. Experiment with incorporating darlings into your poem as appropriate, and note how this influences the trajectory of your poem.

Archive your evolution. Another approach to darlings management is to save multiple versions of a single poem. My friend Lohren Green always has ten or more previous drafts trailing behind a final poem on subsequent Microsoft Word document pages. In addition to retrospectively helping him track how a poem has evolved, this precise record lets Lohren refer back to, reconsider, and sometimes reinstate language that has been cut. When I revise, I like to save each version of a poem in a different Word document (such as "Alchemy 1," "Alchemy 2," "Alchemy 3," etc.). Whatever format you choose, having easily accessible versions of your poems makes it easy to retrieve what's been lost along the way. It can also help you be more liberal with your edits when you're not afraid of losing some possibility forever.

71

LISTS AS TRIGGERS

The poet Tess Gallagher had an interesting entry exam for her first poetry workshop. Potential students were given this list of words from which they were to compose a poem: *bruise, horse, milk, reason,* and *bride.* Gallagher made each word her own, invented surprising, fresh images, and wrote her way right into that class.

THE HORSE IN THE DRUGSTORE | BY TESS GALLAGHER

wants to be admired.
He no longer thinks of what he has given up
to stand here, the milk-white reason
of chickens over his head in the night, the grass
spilling on through the day. No, it is enough
to stand so with his polished chest among the nipples
and bibs, the cotton, and multiple sprays, with his black lips
parted just slightly and the forehooves doubled back
in the lavender air. He has learned when maligned to snort
dimes and to carry the inscrutable bruise like a bride.

As we can see in this poem, lists can offer interesting opportunities to force our hand—and imagination—into shaping unexpected narrative. We can choose a stable of words or phrases as place markers, then find a way to embrace or navigate around them. Think of a list poem as a linguistic obstacle course that challenges you to find new ways out of the old maze.

I once witnessed the poet Casey Bush reading a poem comprised entirely of a list of fortune-cookie fortunes. It's a brilliant collection of non-sequitur wisdom, humorous advice, and delightful English-as-a-second-language-isms all jumbled together in a way that is so engaging that I remember it years after that first listening.

The poet Dorianne Laux has a series of poems that began as challenges from her husband, poet Joseph Millar, to integrate a series of disparate and difficult words into successful poems. At a live reading, after awing us with the finished poem, she offered the foundational words to the audience. It was interesting to consider how a topic, theme, or series of images might rise up around a handful of gawky gifts we are given, to make their own kind of music.

What do you collect? What kinds of lists do you keep? What kinds of lists would be fun to start developing in pursuit of a poem?

TRY THIS!

- Write a poem using the words first presented to Tess Gallagher: *bruise, horse, milk, reason,* and *bride.* Make them your own. See how many surprising ideas and associations you can wring out of these common words.

- Find a list you have lying around your house: a shopping list, to-do list, to-read list—the more ordinary the better. Write the items on your list into a poem and see where it takes you.

- Choose your favorite five words from the poem below. Write them down. Now use them in your own poem, telling a completely different story, in an altogether alternative context.

MEDITATIONS AT LAGUNITAS | BY ROBERT HASS

All the new thinking is about loss.
In this it resembles all the old thinking.
The idea, for example, that each particular erases
the luminous clarity of a general idea. That the
        clown-
faced woodpecker probing the dead sculpted trunk
of that black birch is, by his presence,
some tragic falling off from a first world
of undivided light. Or the other notion that,
because there is in this world no one thing
to which the bramble of blackberry corresponds,
a word is elegy to what it signifies.
We talked about it late last night and in the voice
of my friend, there was a thin wire of grief, a tone
almost querulous. After a while I understood that,
talking this way, everything dissolves: justice,
pine, hair, woman, you and I. There was a woman
I made love to and I remembered how, holding
her small shoulders in my hands sometimes,
I felt a violent wonder at her presence
like a thirst for salt, for my childhood river
with its island willows, silly music from the
        pleasure boat,
muddy places where we caught the little orange-
        silver fish
called pumpkinseed. It hardly had to do with her.
Longing, we say, because desire is full
of endless distances. I must have been the same
        to her.
But I remember so much, the way her hands
        dismantled bread,
the thing her father said that hurt her, what
she dreamed. There are moments when the body is
        as numinous
as words, days that are the good flesh continuing.
Such tenderness, those afternoons and evenings,
saying blackberry, blackberry, blackberry.

ღ 72 ღ

REJECTION HAPPENS

*"No one can make you feel inferior without
your consent."*

—Eleanor Roosevelt

A friend sent me an e-mail. It went something like this:

> "I sent three poems out to a bunch of literary
> journals. I think I shot too high. The rejec-
> tions are a rollin' in. How to cope? Now I hate
> those three poems. Not good to be so thin
> skinned, huh?"

I could have written this e-mail. You could have written it. Anyone who writes poems and sends them out to journals for consideration has had her hopes dashed, her poems rejected, and her faith in her poetic prowess blasted to smithereens. For most of us, this has happened too many times to count.

The common wisdom is that you should develop a thick skin, but I disagree. If you were thick skinned, you would probably be playing football or running for office rather than writing poetry. Just as a cell wall is selectively permeable to take in nutrients, a poet must also be selectively permeable to allow the pains and pleasures of Life On Earth to penetrate. For many of us, learning how to live with extreme sensitivities brought us to poetry in the first place.

So, how do you manage the pain of rejection? Here are a few ideas.

- **Always have the next batch ready.** Because Natalie Gold-berg said so, I have religiously followed this advice. When a

231

rejection letter comes—as they often do—you will have one simple, emotionally detached, task that keeps you moving forward. I cannot emphasize enough how important this is. Get that next submission envelope in the mail, and then you can deal with the disappointment of the rejection. In the meanwhile, you'll be moving forward without letting discouragement create interference.

- **Focus on the success of sending out your work.** Whereas most people look at publication as the end goal of sending out their work, I focus on getting the envelope in the mail as my big achievement. Since that's the only part of the publication process that I have any control over, I really congratulate myself on doing my part!

- **Don't take it personally.** The pursuit of publishing has the potential to provoke a crisis of faith in your work. Rejections put you face-to-face with your vulnerability. While editors do have the authority to publish or reject your work, they are just people with subjective opinions like the rest of us. There is no telling what administrative, political, personal, or act-of-nature influences inform any publication's acceptance decisions. It's best not to invest energy or imagination in how or why such conclusions come to be.

- **Get rejected more often.** You can't win the lottery if you don't play the lottery. And you can't publish your poems if you don't send them out. The more acclimated you get to the boomerang of sending your work out and having it returned, the less monumental each rejection will become. With time and repetition, the mountains of rejection in your mind will shrink to molehills, to be easily stepped over and moved beyond.

- **Celebrate your rejections.** I keep each year's rejection letters in their own file folder. As the folder fattens, I pride myself in sending my work out to so many places. In my early twenties, I had a friend who papered a bulletin board with rejection letters; he looked to this board for inspiration whenever

WRITING THE LIFE POETIC

he wanted to challenge himself to strive further. For fun, he and his housemates would occasionally throw darts at the board to show those rejections who was the boss!

- **Love your poems anyway.** Whether or not anyone else ever sees it this way, my poems have great worth to me. Each poem arose to help me make sense of some aspect of my life, and serves as a small place marker along my path. The companionship and understanding that I am able to give myself through poetry have value that cannot be measured by publication or any other external validation. Articulate what you love about writing poems, and this will help you return to center when you find yourself knocked off course.

- **Collect evidence.** You certainly don't need other people's approval, but it's always nice. Why not accumulate evidence that makes a case for your poetry's value in the eyes of your community? Keep a file or list of positive feedback you receive from friends, family, classmates, and neighbors to remind yourself that your poetry has an audience to whom it matters.

LAST NIGHT, AS I WAS SLEEPING
(EXCERPT) | BY ANTONIO MACHADO, TRANSLATED BY ROBERT BLY

Last night, as I was sleeping,
I dreamt—marvelous error!—
that I had a beehive
here inside my heart.
And the golden bees
were making white combs
and sweet honey
from my old failures.

⟊ 73 ⟊

NATIONAL POETRY MONTH

Did you know that April is National Poetry Month? In communities everywhere, good folks like you and I come together to celebrate poetry. Chances are good that if you're in a somewhat metropolitan area, you'll be able to find readings, events, lectures, and other good poetry fun in abundance throughout the month of April. I invite you to participate in at least three poetry events this coming April. Make sure that you do the one that sounds the most fun and the one that sounds the strangest. If there's an opportunity to participate—often readings are followed by open mics—be prepared to do your part and get up there and be brave! The rest of the folks shaking in their boots will be grateful.

Of course, not everyone has access to such events where they live—either because of a limited selection of activities or limited time and flexibility. But I propose that if those wild NaNoWriMo (National Novel Writing Month) fiction writers can crank out an entire novel in the month of November, you can surely find the time to get out there and make April a month of poetry—with or without the infrastructure of community activities. Here are a few ideas for making National Poetry Month your own.

TRY THIS!

- Photocopy your favorite poem (your own or someone else's) and mail it to all of your favorite people.

- Take a night off (or day or weekend—as much time as you can possibly afford) where you're not responsible for dinner, kids, laundry, work, or being well behaved. Eat something indulgent, sit in a bubble bath, and read a book of poetry out loud by candlelight.

- Listen to a recording of poets reading—online, on DVD or CD (see chapter forty-five for a list of online listening resources). Shoot for a mix of poets you know you enjoy and at least a few you've never heard of before.

- Sign up to receive a daily poem by e-mail from The Writer's Almanac With Garrison Keillor (http://writersalmanac.publicradio.org). It's free, it's easy, and it sure is delightful to have poems chosen for you and delivered like a little gift to your inbox every day.

- Host a poetry circle in your home. Combine it with a meal, if you like. Invite friends to spend an evening sharing their favorite poems. Vary this by reading and discussing your own poetry in addition to the work of others. Notice and comment on each other's delivery style. What makes a successful poem reading? What can you learn from each other? What do you notice about the poems you've chosen?

- Participate in an online poetry community. Connect with poets everywhere seeking inspiration, to improve skills, and to share the delight of poetry. A few great examples are:

  - Wild Poetry Forum (www.wildpoetryforum.com)
  - Poem Online (http://poem.org/blog)
  - Writing the Life Poetic (www.writingthelifepoetic. typepad.com)

- Create a free poetry stand in your front yard. Get a real estate sign (the kind that has a slot for flyers in it) and install it in your front yard. Instead of house-for-sale flyers, fill the little compartment every week with copies of a different poem. Decorate the sign in a way that makes it clear that you're offering a gift of poetry to passersby.

- Do a guerilla poetry blitz. Create a little zine of your poems and make a hundred copies. (Be sure to include an e-mail address so folks can share their delight with you when they find your zine.) Leave them in cafés, libraries, bookstores, and other public places where they are likely to be found, read, and enjoyed.

- Declare your own NaPoWriMo (National Poetry Writing Month). Write a poem a day. It doesn't have to be a good poem or a finished poem. Just a poem. Meet up with a friend and drink a lot of coffee if you have to. Call in sick. Leave the dishes in the sink. But write that poem. Day after day after day. Want some good company and inspiration along the way? Visit Poetic Asides (http://blog.writersdigest.com/poeticasides), the blog of Robert Lee Brewer, editor of *Writer's Market*. Brewer hosts a "Poem-a-Day" challenge throughout April, offering prompts and inviting his readers to write a new poem every day. I dare you.

74

From Facts to Truths

"I've found that poetry allows some things to be said that are difficult to say and more difficult to hear. It can provide a framework for bold ideas, what ifs, truth, and revealing. One has many choices, ample opportunities to read across decades and even centuries, learn from poets around the world—and after all that, find the common elements of the human condition."

—Toni Partington

PERSONALIZING HISTORY

Newspapers and history books give us facts. Poems take us inside the emotional truths of an event, that we might make it our own, become a part of it, and comprehend it with more of ourselves than merely our minds. In essence, a poem can offer an opportunity to not just understand a past event but to enter a deeply felt moment of human experience and know it from the inside out. Following is a poem that demonstrates this possibility:

Triangle Shirtwaist Factory Fire | by Robert Phillips

I, Rose Rosenfeld, am one of the workers
who survived. Before the inferno broke out,
factory doors had been locked by the owners,

    to keep us at our sewing machines,
    to keep us from stealing scraps of cloth.

I said to myself, What are the bosses doing?
I knew they would save themselves.

I left my big-button-attacher machine,
climbed the iron stairs to the tenth floor
where their offices were. From the landing window

    I saw girls in shirtwaists flying by,
    Catherine wheels projected like Zeppelins
    out open windows, then plunging downward,
    sighing skirts open parasols on fire.

I found the big shots stuffing themselves
into the freight elevator going to the roof.
I squeezed in. While our girls were falling,

    we ascended like ashes. Firemen
    yanked us onto the next-door roof.
    I sank to the tarpaper, sobbed for
    one-hundred forty-six comrades dying

or dead down below. One was Rebecca,
my only close friend, a forewoman kind to workers.
Like the others, she burned like a prism.

    Relatives of twenty-three victims later
      Brought suits.
    Each family was awarded seventy-five dollars.
    It was like the *Titanic* the very next year—
    No one cared about the souls in steerage.

Those doors were locked, too, a sweatshop at sea.
They died due to ice, not fire. I live in
Southern California now. But I still see

    skirts rippling like parachutes,
    girls hit the cobblestones, smell smoke,
    burnt flesh, girls cracking like cheap buttons,
    disappearing like so many dropped stitches.

Reading accounts of this event from other sources, we can glean factual information, such as: the sequence of misjudgments that led to this disaster, the politics of the time that made it possible, and the number of deaths. Whereas this poem invites us to participate in the event through Rose Rosenfeld's lens, as imagined and shared by the poet.

ENCOUNTERING YOUR OWN CONSCIENCE

Poetry doesn't often strive to teach us an objective or moral right from wrong. Rather, it may be instructive about what's right and wrong for us.

DEER SEASON | BY BARBARA TANNER ANGELL

My sister and her friend, Johnny Morley,
used to go on Saturdays to the Bancroft Hotel
to visit his grandfather.

One autumn, the beginning of deer season,
the old man told them,

"Used to hunt when I was a boy,
woods all around here then,
but I never went again after that time . . .

the men went out, took me with them,
and I shot my first buck.
It was wounded, lying in the leaves,

so they told me,
take the pistol, shoot it in the head.
I went straight up to it,
looked right into its eyes.

Just before I pulled the trigger,
it licked my hand."

This poem, for example, doesn't advise that hunting is good or bad. It presents the emotional truth of hunting for this particular speaker and lets the reader draw her own conclusions.

EXPRESSING HIGHER KINDNESS

I was raised with the expression, "Sticks and stones may break my bones, but names can never hurt me." Like most things I was told about life, this proverb turned out to be wildly inadequate in summarizing the complex ways in which we damage each other and ourselves. Bones heal. But names we take in. Most of us carry into adulthood any number of unkind words that have become lodged in our softest places. Inside of us, hidden so as to protect us from further pain, these words gain momentum: *Ugly, fat, stupid, loser.*

In his book, *The Hidden Messages in Water,* Dr. Masaru Emoto explores how water molecules change under the influence of words. He effectively illustrates that thoughts and feelings affect physical reality. By producing different focused intentions through written and spoken words and music presented to the same water samples, he has been able to document how water changes its expression.

For example, water that has been exposed to nourishing words (I checked out *love* and *gratitude*) shows brilliant, complex, colorful snowflake patterns. *Love* looked like an enormous diamond. In contrast, water exposed to negative words (*defeat, rage, despair*) form incomplete, asymmetrical patterns with dull colors. The water crystal influenced by heavy metal music looked to me like the head of a cymbal.

Given that our bodies are composed of three-fourths water, could this mean that we are also three-fourths susceptible to the influence of words? Perhaps, then, we are what we say.

Poetry cultivates in us an attention to and respect for language that has the potential to make us better citizens. When we can say what we really mean, we can connect better with others and ourselves.

75

TO THINE OWN SELF BE TRUE

Ren was a massage practitioner treating my dog Hamachi for back pain. He had paw prints tattooed around his wrists and Pat Benatar's name running up the inside of his forearm. The first time he came to my house, I found myself singing for the rest of the day in my most macho rocker girl swagger: "You can cry tough baby, it's alright; You can let me down easy, but not tonight."

Ren's second visit inspired, "Before I put another notch in my lipstick case, you better make sure you put me in my place." "Fire and Ice," of course, was simply inevitable.

On his third visit, I asked Ren: "How has it impacted your life to have Pat Benatar's name on your body?"

He was sitting on the floor with Hamachi in his lap. She was upside down, spread eagle, licking his wrists. He was working on softening the fascia of her belly that connects to the spine. He lit up.

"Pat Benatar is my talisman," Ren explained. "Her name on my arm is a daily reminder of who I am and how I want to live. I go into people's homes, and they see her name on my arm, and they are reminded of whom they are and how they want to live. It gets us talking about what matters to us."

I am intrigued by this idea of taking the name or idea or embodiment of someone or something else literally into your skin. Living alongside your life, these words perhaps provide a kind of parallel perception; a harmony playing counterpart to the main melody of your form and function—an aspiration or value to which you have assigned yourself, against which the beating of your own heart aligns or collides.

I have never been certain enough about the longevity of any word, phrase, or belief to tattoo it onto my body. However, I did wear a necklace pendant for maybe three years straight that said, "To thine own self be true." I liked to think of that necklace having powers akin to Wonder Woman's groovy metal bracelets: deflecting all that might steer me off the course of my greatest good. And I am absolutely convinced that those words worked!

Over my desk hangs a framed piece of art that my mother gave me maybe twenty years ago that has been held close in every home since. It reads: "The act of writing is the art of discovering what you believe." —David Hare. Magnetized to the white board I use to track my deadlines are two SARK cards that my friend Pam sent me. One reads "Breathe" and the other, "All your dreams are already coming true." Again: none of these are imprinted on my skin, but all are a part of my daily visual cues as I look up to seek poems from that vast, diaphanous place above my head where they materialize.

Words can be like arrows, focusing your attention in certain directions. And they can be like steering wheels, literally influencing the choices you make and actions you take. I encourage you to think (and feel) carefully about the words you keep close: on your body, where you sleep, work, and live. Sooner or later, the words you see will become a part of your framework of belief. If "Pat Benatar" are the two words you need to keep in sight to remind you of your true North, then by all means become one with the legendary rocker. Whatever it is you believe or you'd like to believe, experiment with letting words be the current that can keep your circuits juiced with your own truth.

TRY THIS!

- Make a word for the year, write it in pretty colors, and hang it in your line of sight. My 2007 word was "Enough!" and my 2008 word was "Receive!" Both are colored in magic marker on index cards, with pretty little hand-drawn designs around them, and are quite visible on the bulletin board in my office, where I see them every day. Both years answered the call of their assigned theme—and then some. What might yours do?

- Ally McBeal said that everyone needs a theme song, and I agree. We measure time with music. We measure relationships with music. We often find ourselves imprinted with the sound tracks that accompany proms and deaths and births and marriages. Choose a theme song, or write your own. Sing it whenever you need to be reminded of the messages therein.

- Write something incredibly important on your hand or arm—somewhere where you'll be able to see and refer to it often. Rewrite it every day if you need to. See what it's like to live with this word or message physically integrated with you.

- Write down one invitation, inspiring quote, or intriguing phrase for yourself every week, and be creative about how you make it visible. Send yourself text message reminders, make it your computer's screen saver, or tape it to the bathroom mirror or the refrigerator.

ALLOW FALLOW TIME

Nature has four distinct cycles. No matter how lofty we might imagine ourselves to be, poets are subject to the laws of nature like every other living thing.

Yet, despite a lifetime of witnessing the world around us bud, blossom, drop petals, push out lush fruit, ripen, burn glorious autumn flames of color, lose everything, slumber, and then start over, we seem to expect of ourselves a nonstop cycle of bud, blossom, fruit, harvest, repeat. (This is not surprising, since this is how the clockwork of our culture turns: to produce, produce, and produce some more.) But the fact is that the flora and fauna don't work that way, and neither do we.

It's simply not natural or sustainable to continuously produce. Farmers rotate their planting so that the land can replenish after a harvest. Poets who want to make the most of their natural resources will make similar choices. One of the great blessings of not being paid to produce poetry is that you are not beholden to supervisors, stockholders, or customers. This means you get to decide how, when, and where you write. You can clock in and clock out if that's what works for you. But I recommend finding a way to align your process with the natural world and learn from the seasons how to trust the cycles of your writing.

Some years ago, author Alice Walker was given a grant to write; she proceeded to move out to the country where she spent a year knitting. As she knit, the characters in *The Color Purple* made themselves known to her, and the force of the story's narrative gathered like rain clouds. I'm guessing that by the time Walker sat down with pen to paper, a veritable storm of a narrative poured forth. When it came time for harvest, readers had the good fortune to pluck *The Color Purple* ripe from the virtual vine.

I remember the first time I heard this story about Alice Walker's writing process. I wondered if she worried, as I have, when she was "doing nothing" that nothing was happening. I wondered if the people around her were anxious that there was no sign of a book being written during that year. Clearly, this is an author who understood far more than I did about embracing and moving with her own cycles and the cycles of nature.

Had Walker sat down with pen in hand every day of that year and forced herself to write according to a regimented schedule, *The Color Purple* may not have had the fallow time it needed to gather force, take shape, and burst forth into the great gust of narrative that made it the story that it is today. You may be compromising your spirit and your poetry in similar ways if you push through a fallow time with forced writing. There's a time for filling the well, and there's a time for drawing from that well to fill your inspiration cup to overflowing.

I'm not proposing that you match what the seasons are doing exactly by writing furiously all spring and summer, then spending the winter canning and preserving all of your good ideas. But I am suggesting that you have a four-part rhythm that's worth exploring so you can better understand when your high productivity times are, when it's time to tend the garden, and when it's time to rest.

PLANTING

For poets, planting time involves accumulating and sinking seeds of poetic possibilities—in whatever way works best for you. You may seek unprecedented experiences, plan travel or interpersonal adventures, spend intimate time in nature, take classes and workshops, read instructional and inspiring books, or attend readings.

NEW GROWTH

This is your time of high-potency writing. Write like the wind. Then write some more! Don't worry about being perfect. It's more important to be receptive and allow in what is knocking at your door. This is a time when you'll want notebooks, index cards, Post-it notes—whatever works for you—everywhere so you don't let a drop of inspiration go to waste.

HARVEST

Harvest is the time of sculpting your raw genius into polished, finished poems. In this phase, the original impulse of the poem finds (with your capable guidance) just the right shape, form, style, and language to manifest most completely.

DORMANCY

This, dear poets, is when you do (what appears to be) absolutely nothing that specifically relates to the production of poetry. You rest. You have fun. You call your mother. You don't worry if you'll ever write another poem again; of course you will! In fact, the less you pay attention to them, the more enthusiastically your poems will be lining up at your door, awaiting a sign from you the way high-school boys get interested in girls the minute it looks like they've found a better alternative. Rest up; you're going to have your hands full when planting time rolls around again!

Just Do It

> *"Just write. I know it sounds cliché or simplistic,*
> *but nothing else will teach you to write. You can*
> *take a million classes, read a thousand books,*
> *but the only way to learn is to put your hand to*
> *paper or the keyboard and get started. Imagine*
> *a novice baker who read all the cookbooks in the*
> *world but never made a cake. So, just write. If*
> *it falls flat or gets burnt the first, and hundredth,*
> *time, that's okay. It might not feel like it, but*
> *you're getting better each time."*
>
> —Shanna Germain

Poet Ted Kooser says that in a strategy engineered to impress the girls as a young man, he called himself a poet and carried around large, impressive books to prove it. After a few years, it occurred to him that if he was going to be a poet, he'd better start writing poems. And so he did—to much eventual critical acclaim.

This seems to be a common phenomenon: People fancy themselves poets without doing the work of writing poems because this reflection appeals to them. I don't particularly object to this approach; a poet is as worthy an ideal as any I've ever come across. And as was the case with Kooser, maybe the combination of identifying as a poet and carrying around a few fabulous props are all you'll need to grease the wheels of your own poetic process . . . such that one day you awaken and find yourself writing poems!

I've also observed the opposite: people who have been writing poems passionately, but privately, for years and never think to call themselves a poet. Some believe that the identity of "poet" is earned only via publication or public recognition. It's no surprise that we hold ourselves in this light, since this is largely how the outer world judges and validates poets: We are deemed legitimate once we have something to show in the way of commerce. I noticed among my own community of wonderful, supportive friends and family (who had little experience with or understanding of poetry) a significant shift in regard for me when I was granted a fellowship to study poetry in a graduate creative writing program. Suddenly, because a large and respectable institution said that my poetry was worthy of a financial reward, there seemed to be consensus that I was A Poet.

Having the support of one's community is nice, and being paid to study and write poetry is even better. But neither of these can make or break a poet. As I see it, poets are simply people who write poems. There is no special badge required, no institution necessary to give you it's blessing. Truly, there is no prerequisite other than desire. Nothing but desire will keep you coming back to the page to work and rework and work some more at cultivating language into that exquisite container of a poem.

How you choose to identify is up to you. How much you write is up to you. But if you've enjoyed getting acquainted with poetry and are considering a long-term relationship, I advise you to keep those sleeves rolled up and your hands dirty. There's nothing like falling into a poem to keep you receptive and attentive to what is broken open inside you. There's nothing like writing through a poem to teach you how to inhabit what is whole.

"Lover's Leap" (excerpt) by Martha Beck

A Jewish friend told me this story: A man asks his rabbi, "Why does God write the law on our hearts? Why not in our hearts? It's the inside of my heart that needs God." The rabbi answered, "God never forces anything into a human heart. He writes the word on our hearts so that when our hearts break, God falls in." Whatever you hold sacred, you'll find that an unguarded broken heart is the ideal instrument for absorbing it.

If you fall into intimacy without resistance, despite your alarm, either you will fall into love, which is exquisite, or love will fall into you, which is more exquisite still. Do it enough, and you may just lose your fear of falling. You'll get better at missing the ground, at keeping a crushed heart open so that love can find all the broken pieces. And the next time you feel that vertiginous sensation of the floor disappearing, even as your reflexes tell you to duck and grab, you'll hear an even deeper instinct saying, "Fall in! Fall in!"

Ꙩ 78 Ꙩ

KEEPING YOUR WILDERNESS ALIVE

"Solitude is the sense of space as nourishing. What usually happens with solitude is that people equate it with loneliness, which frightens them ... There is a way in which we treat our relationships almost like a colonial expedition: we want to colonize the space, all the territory in between, until there is no wilderness left. Most couples who have deadened in each other's presence have colonized their space this way. They have domesticated each other beyond recognition."

—John O'Donohue

On a Saturday morning, Jon dropped me off at yoga class at ten A.M. and kept right on driving with the dogs to Forest Park where they galloped six muddy miles of trail together in the deep womb of urban wilderness. I had dressed for the walk home, and was warm and relaxed as I headed out from class into the mild gloom of a March afternoon. Digging around in my purse to no avail, it struck me that we had used my keys in the car, and that the car—and keys—were with Jon; I'd be locked out until he returned. Jon didn't have his phone with him, and I had no idea when he would be home.

With destination erased from my trajectory, I felt like a balloon cut free, floating purposeless and weightless down Clinton Street. I remembered seeing a café on my way to class and walked east another three blocks to Broder, a Scandinavian café. The café was long and narrow, about the size of a train car, and had been polished with care to a modern minimalist sheen. The patrons had clearly emerged from a Portland other than the one I inhabit: one of high-style, where darkly framed, dramatic eyegear and strangely proportioned clothes in shades of black and brown slung over heroin-chic bony bodies. The waiters and chefs were waify, underweight young men smattered with tattoos and too-tight black pants with a slick of aloofness greasing down the errant eagerness beneath their cool façades. In my sloppy stretch pants, bunched-down wool socks, fleece jacket, and unwashed hair flopping around in a loose clip, I was blissfully out of place. In an urban environment, not looking the part is as close to invisible as you get, and I love being invisible.

I took a seat at the bar, retrieved a small pile of index cards and a pen from my purse, and started writing. Card after card, the ideas kept coming through me, through the pen. A practice established over the course of twenty years, my body needed only assume the position to turn on its free writing tap. As I wrote, a glorious mug of fragrant decaf coffee arrived with a smart glass jar of sugar cubes and a silver carafe of half and half. Then came the large, frothy orange juice. And then three aebleskivers, quarter-size Danish pancakes dusted in powdered sugar and circled in dollops of lingonberry jam, maple syrup, and lemon curd. Compliments of the chef. I had fallen through the rabbit hold to a Swedish heaven.

As I wrote, my baked scramble with wild mushrooms and caramelized onions materialized on the counter steaming in its square, cast-iron baking dish, aligned with a square white plate with a perfectly spiced potato pancake accompanied by a fan of triangular slices of walnut bread. I tasted, marveled, and wrote some more. And as I did, I was transported to the life and times of Sage of yesteryear. This Sage had free time. With little income and minimal expenses, she lived for the indulgence of her weekend café breakfasts. With no car but plenty of notebooks and one divine poetry book at a time, she'd ride the streetcar and listen and look and feel and write and weep. This old Sage was spontaneous. Not yet the precariously over-committed and over-scheduled adult she would grow up to be, this young woman had room for surprises.

For a brief hour of homelessness and exquisite food, I returned to this lost wilderness of my early twenties: the Sage of open spaces. I carried her home like a pressed flower—fragile and old and new. In a flash of lucidity, I could see how I had colonized myself into my own prison of responsibility and purpose and civic duty as year after year I cut back the rich, fertile thrill of my precious solitude to cultivate a more groomed and professional version of myself. When really all I wanted was something big and impossible and gloriously alive to get lost in.

Poetry does not survive the suburbs we make of our minds. It withers in the cage of constant accomplishment. Poetry needs the wilderness of solitude to call itself up out of the verdant ashes. It needs the darkness and the light to recognize its wholeness. How have you colonized your creativity and domesticated that wildflower of your imagination that once billowed in the wind? How will you recover your lost wilderness? No matter what work you do, what relationship you have, or how busy you are, inch by inch it can be done. You can have your suburbs and your wilderness. Your poetry depends on it.

How to Run a Reading Series

If you'd like to get intimately involved with your local literary community, running a reading series is a great way to make a big impact without a tremendous amount of work. The most important ingredient in launching a reading series is the passionate desire to do so. Administrative skills help, as does being at least somewhat extroverted. Following are a few key steps that every curator should have on her to-do list.

DEFINE YOUR EVENT

How often do you want the reading series to meet? (Monthly? Quarterly?) What do you want the duration of the event to be? (I recommend no more than an hour; that's about as long as an audience can take in poetry without getting restless.) How do you want to structure the format? (Three featured poets, each reading for twenty minutes? One featured poet reading for half an hour, then an open mic for the second half? An open mic for the hour? Poets and fiction writers? Poets only? A spoken word competition?) Get a clear picture of how you want the event to run so you can communicate that clearly when inviting folks to read.

ESTABLISH RELATIONSHIPS

Reading series are about community. If you don't have an existing writing community, start building one. Attend readings, workshops, conferences, lectures, poetry slams, writing groups—whatever pleases you and brings you closer to like-minded literary types. This is a great way to start cultivating a stable of poets you can invite to read and an audience of listeners passionate about poetry. If you're shy about schmoozing or would like alternative community-building channels, try advertising for readers online via Craigslist (www.craigslist.org), literary listservs, and blogs. Strive to line up readers for the first three events before you even get started.

CHOOSE A VENUE

Identify a venue that reflects the feeling of the event you want to host: a library, bar, bookstore, corporate conference room, coffee shop, theater, dance studio, or performance space could all work fine. The two most important factors are that you feel comfortable in the space, and that the venue is pleased to have your event there. Depending on the size of the venue and your expected audience size, a microphone and podium may also be key to your negotiations.

In general, businesses that benefit from extra foot traffic would be the most interested in hosting a reading. And while it is possible that a venue might be willing to pay you to host your event there, it is more likely that you will be able to arrange for a free drink, a small discount, or some other kind of perk for the readers.

Choose a regular meeting time that works well for the venue and you and is easy for participants to remember, such as the first Wednesday of every month.

A note of warning: Make sure to negotiate with your venue the option to have poets sell their books and chapbooks at the event. For some larger bookstores, this may not be an option. It's good to know what's possible at the front end, as it may influence your venue choice.

PUBLICIZE

Here's a quickie timeline of to-do's:

1. **Before you do anything else:** Make a media contact list of all literary arts editors at your local city, town, and neighborhood newspapers and newsletters, radio stations, community e-mail lists, writing associations, etc.

2. **Two months before each reading:** Line up poets from the event and gather bios and headshot photos from them.

3. **Six weeks before each reading:** Write a press release about the event and distribute it to your media list and featured

poets. (E-mail is a fast, efficient, and popular way to distribute press releases.)

4. **A month before each reading, and then again a week before the reading:** Send an e-mail blast to your "reading series" list to invite them to the upcoming event. If your budget allows, you could also mail postcard invites and post flyers for the event in public spaces such as libraries, cafés, and grocery stores.

5. **A week before each reading:** Remind scheduled readers of the event logistics: time, place, reading order, and what you'd like from them (such as, "Don't forget to bring books to sell! Please be prepared to read for twenty minutes and then sign books at the end of the reading"). Confirm with the venue that they're expecting you on the day and at the time for which your event is scheduled.

BUILD IT AND THEY WILL COME

When you present great writers and make listeners feel welcome and comfortable, your community will likely gain a steady momentum. Always bring an e-mail sign-up sheet so you can bring new people into the fold. At the end of each reading, thank your readers, thank your audience, thank the venue, and announce the date of your next event—as well as the featured readers for that event. Over time, your series will take on a life of its own—with readers referring other readers, and listeners bringing other listeners.

I started a reading series three years ago from scratch, not knowing a single literary person in my community. Today, I have three readers per month booked out a year in advance. Within six months, I was on autopilot with my promotions, scheduling, and planning so that now the whole shebang only takes a few hours every month. The reading series keeps me motivated to find, listen to, and support great poets in my community.

๑ 80 ๑

FLAP YOUR WINGS!

My friend Christina Katz has encouraged me over the past few years to take on many exciting, new poetic challenges, including writing this book. Recently, I said to her with reverence: "Thank you for pushing me out of the nest!"

"Oh, you had already jumped out of the nest," she assured me. "I was just shouting, 'Flap your wings, flap your wings!'"

By now, you're flapping your wings, too! In these eighty chapters, we've covered a wide range of poetry craft, process, and content development possibilities. And we've explored ways to get inspired and stay inspired while living and writing a life poetic. You may even know a little more about what poetry means to you, how it informs your relationship with yourself and the world, and why you enjoy writing it.

Poetry is a natural resource that will always be available to you. You don't need any expensive instruments to write it or share it. And you don't need intimidating classes to learn it. Your love of language, your willingness to experiment, and your passion for discovery are enough to establish a poetry practice that can sustain you for the rest of your life. Perhaps you have found a few road signs here that have pointed you down paths you'd like to travel. If you continue to invite them, you will find an abundance of cues in your everyday life that disclose new paths and trigger new poems.

It is said that Ruth Stone describes her experience of channeling poetry as a great wind coming through. When she feels the first tremors of turbulence in the grass, she races home to pen and paper in hopes of capturing the great gust of language before it disperses and is lost. Your job as a poet is much the same: to stay open to what is coming through, to learn how to recognize the language that has chosen you and then write it down.

My hope is that this book serves as a creative companion for the little jumps and big leaps along the way as your poetry writing practice takes flight. If you'd like more interactive companionship, visit Writing the Life Poetic online at www.writingthelifepoetic.com and www.writingthelifepoetic.typepad.com, where poets working with this book are learning and practicing together. Share your poems and your thoughts along the way with other people writing the life poetic.

Leaving the nest of the familiar to try something new is always risky. Congratulations on stretching beyond your comfort zone into the wide, wild wonder of poetry! Enjoy the ride, and don't forget: Flap your wings, flap your wings!

INDEX

ACKNOWLEDGMENTS

This book would not exist without the encouragement and example of Christina Katz. She helped me recognize my platform and value my expertise; then she challenged me to share both with a wider audience. From pitch to polish, Christina was my North Star. My editor, Jane Friedman, worked with me to sculpt vision into form. With her expert guidance, this book found its center and its sense of direction. I am extremely fortunate to have Grégoire Vion's illustrations resonating throughout these pages. His work harmonizes with my words to create a greater poetry than I could achieve alone. Pamela Kim, my creative co-conquistadora for more than a decade, has been invaluable at every stage of this book's conception and development—as sounding board, brainstormer, cheerleader, and proofreader. I owe a great deal to my poetry community, many of who have generously shared their wisdom and insights here. Special thanks to Mari L'Esperance for many years of poetic friendship, Sebastian Ellis for being an enthusiastic and honest reader, Nicole Davis for teaching me the wabi sabi art of repurposing, and Paulann Petersen, Master Poet, for her gracious service to Portland poets. My parents, Bobbi Cohen and Bryan Cohen, share a love of language that informed my own. They have always encouraged my creativity and given me every possible opportunity to develop my mind, heart, and soul. My husband, Jonathan Luchs, has brought so much happiness, metaphor, and mood lighting to our home. He cooked all the meals and washed all the dishes to give me the space and time to write this book. My son, Theo Luchs-Cohen, who was conceived and birthed alongside this book, is my daily meditation on the life poetic. Humbly, I thank my patron saints Henry, Hamachi, Valentino, and Diablo. These beloved dogs and cats share with me their open-hearted days and nights; I am a better person for it.

ABOUT THE AUTHOR

Sage Cohen is the author of the poetry collection *Like the Heart, the World*. Her poems and essays have appeared in dozens of publications including *The Sunday Oregonian, Poetry Flash, Oregon Literary Review, VoiceCatcher,* and *Greater Good*. In 2008 she was nominated for a Pushcart Prize, and in 2006 she won first prize in the Ghost Road Press poetry contest. Sage teaches poetry e-courses and writes a monthly column about the life poetic for *Writers on the Rise*, where she also serves as Managing Editor. A speaker at writing conferences, festivals, bookstores and libraries, she hosts the Barnes & Noble Reading Series in Portland, Oregon. To learn more about Sage, visit www.writingthelifepoetic.com.

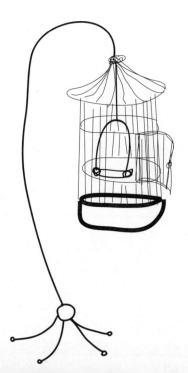